IF YOU

WOULD BE

HAPPY

Ruth Stout

Martino Fine Books
Eastford, CT
2021

Martino Fine Books
P.O. Box 913,
Eastford, CT 06242 USA

ISBN   978-1-68422-594-1

Copyright 2021

Martino Fine Books

All rights reserved. No new contribution to this publication may
be reproduced, stored in a retrieval system, or transmitted, in any form
or by any means, electronic, mechanical, photocopying, recording, or
otherwise, without the prior permission of the Publisher.

Cover Design Tiziana Matarazzo

Printed in the United States of America On 100% Acid-Free Paper

IF YOU

WOULD BE

HAPPY

Ruth Stout

DOUBLEDAY & COMPANY, INC., GARDEN CITY, N. Y. 1962

Copyright © 1962 by Ruth Stout
All Rights Reserved
Printed in the United States of America

For everyone under ninety—
after that you're on your own.

IF YOU WOULD BE HAPPY

I

Some Common Sense Will Come in Handy

Shall we, quick, before the pursuit of happiness becomes an outmoded goal, see what we can do about snaring a little for ourselves? Well, before we do anything else, let's unhitch our wagon from that star; that uplifting thought is too impractical, for not only is it unlikely that we will make much headway, but also I doubt if we will even get a decent start.

We need only translate that attractive notion into realistic terms to see how fragile it is. Imagine some little boys who want to find out how far they can run without stopping; you might conceivably manage to persuade them to try for a five-mile goal, but if you suggested that perhaps they could run all the way from Maine to California without a stop, I doubt if they would undertake it. They might even think you weren't serious.

Stars are bright and shining, but for humans they are at present out of reach. They may inspire us to write a poem, or a symphony, or to think noble if fleeting thoughts, but they don't stand by us when the dentist tells us that tooth has to come out, or the boss gets unreasonable and fires us.

It can be an uplifting experience to wander along a babbling brook in early morning, to listen to the birds and all the mysterious sounds around us, to breathe in the freshness, and, with our wagon hitched to a star, feel that we can get there by leaps and bounds. In this mood a lasting happiness of the highest order seems to be ours for the taking.

I hope everyone has such moments, but the trouble is they come and go—mostly go. In fact, they probably don't last through even one day if somebody nags at us, the children decide not to mind, the landlord raises the rent, the electrician doesn't show up—or, almost worse, he does and overcharges outrageously.

Yesterday I happened to hear a radio program in which a woman was interviewing a man who had written a successful play. It went along innocuously enough, if dully, until for some reason (or more likely for none) the man said something slightly ecstatic about pursuing the unattainable. The interviewer loved that, and said with a rapturous sigh:

"Oh, but don't we *all* pursue the unattainable?"

They decided we all did, and were awfully pleased about it.

Well, I hope they were mistaken. Let's put this, too, into

practical terms. Mr. A is working in his garden; Mr. B comes along and, watching him, is surprised to see that he is carefully planting, not seeds, but a neat row of small stones. He asks Mr. A his reason for this, and finds that the stones are supposed to grow into big flagstones which Mr. A needs for making a walk.

"But that isn't possible," objects Mr. B. "Those stones won't grow."

"Of course not," agrees Mr. A. "But who wants to mess around just pursuing the attainable?"

Working for something which we know beforehand is quite impossible for us to achieve, taken seriously and literally, is for the very young and the insane, with possibly a poet here and there. And if it isn't taken seriously, what good is it? There is a tremendous difference between aiming at something fine which seems almost beyond our reach and something which is without doubt beyond it; the latter surely makes for nothing but frustration.

One effective way to check up on our ideals to find out if they are at all workable, or just a lot of idle talk, is to try them out on a thoughtful and intelligent child before he is befuddled by the discrepancy between what grownups say and what they do. If the playwright went home from that broadcast I mentioned and faced his bright son who had listened in on it, the conversation might go something like this:

"Dad, should everyone pursue the unattainable?"

"Yes, son."

"Should I?"

"Why, yes—yes, of course."

"What does it mean?"

"Well—er—you try to do something or be something which you know is beyond you."

The child is puzzled, and who can blame him? Presently he asks:

"Why? Wouldn't it be better to spend my time trying to do something that maybe I could do?"

Now the father may do some explaining about lofty ideals, but I'm afraid he will still have a perplexed child on his hands. It's an absurd thing to say, and I suppose I don't actually mean it, but it has occurred to me more than once that perhaps children would be lucky if they were deaf for the first several years of their lives and couldn't hear the outlandish things that grownups say, not only to them but to each other.

It is bad enough to load ourselves with ideals we have no expectation of reaching and actually no serious intention of even trying to reach, but we are also making demands on our children which at best are vague, at worst meaningless, because they are completely unrealistic. Take this simple command: "Don't cry, dear." Maybe it's good for him to cry and get it out of his system; in any case, he can't stop automatically just because you tell him to, and he isn't at all interested in trying. Why add another "don't" to the long list on which you aren't going to follow through?

When we children cried Mother would say, "There, there, must you cry so hard? Let's see how *little* you can cry." Now that *was* interesting, and we would begin to experiment and would soon become fascinated at the sound of our sobs growing fainter and fainter.

Mother had nine children, and never in my life did I hear her tell any of us to do something that was beyond our scope of endeavor. Never, for instance, did she issue that absurd command: "Be a good child." Naturally we were good if we could swing it, because we felt better inside and people were nicer to us when we were. It paid off, and we certainly didn't need to be reminded of such an obvious thing. When we weren't good it was because at that particular time we couldn't be, and Mother was intelligent enough to know it.

I suppose that every normal person would like to have a happy, serene, pleasurable life. Many, I should think, if they had just one wish, would ask for happiness. And yet how many of us actually put our minds to it and work for it in a consistent, sensible, determined way?

We take it for granted that we must exert ourselves for everything else. Without questioning it we work for our livelihood, our education, our luxuries, and to learn to become doctors, shoemakers, lawyers, nurses, engineers, stenographers, teachers. We work to earn money to pay for our hair-dos, new cars, movies, television, redecorating the house. We abandon our old clothes, only half worn out, because they are no longer in style and work to earn money to buy new ones. We'll even give some thought, probably spasmodically, to our health and to keeping our weight down. But who ever heard of working consistently, intelligently, every day, for happiness? And why not? Isn't it worth it? Don't we care enough?

How many people do you know who spend time and thought and money scurrying off to some warm and colorful spot in the winter, and to Europe perhaps in the summer?

I know quite a few. And how many who spend anything at all working and planning systematically for happiness? None, I'm afraid. If only advertisers could sell happiness (the real thing) all tied up in gay packages, what a world we would have! Heaven would lose status.

But all this isn't as crazy as it sounds, because people know how to work and save money for a trip to Europe but they don't seem to know how to set about working for happiness. Perhaps it's because our thinking machines get all clogged up in early youth and we are simply swept along with the tide. People will do something definite toward attaining a single pleasure, but who makes detailed plans for a pleasant life all the time, day in, day out? Or for just one uncluttered week? So it doesn't occur to us that happiness is a commodity that, like everything else, has to be planned for and worked for and, better than that, is attainable if we are willing to give it as much attention and thought as we spend on all sorts of trivial and temporary enjoyments.

Nor do we have to sacrifice anything worth while. In the case of other luxuries we may have to choose between two things we want, such as a new suit and a new chair. But the envy, nagging, hurt feelings, and the worry which we will have to abandon when we choose serenity are rubbish, and it is a joy to trade them in for something else.

If we have decided to work seriously for happiness, we can't be casual about it any more than we can get anywhere if we are vague when we undertake to master a trade or skill. If you are beginning to learn to play the piano, you can't think hazily now and then, without doing anything about it, how lovely it would be to play the Chopin Preludes. You'll have to start with scales, and you'll have to practice and keep at it if you are serious about playing Chopin.

I have often been laughed at when I try to teach something I've just begun to study myself. I have never really learned to play the piano, but I once taught what little I knew to my nieces and nephews. I taught gardening as soon as the first radish I planted showed its little sprout aboveground. A friend startled me not long ago by reminding me of the time, years ago, when I taught French to a small group of eager beavers. I had forgotten that and, since my knowledge of French is practically non-existent, was a little shocked and then I thought: Why should I be? If I know that *merci* means "thank you," there's no harm in telling someone, is there? Needless to say, I don't charge for that kind of teaching.

With such a background, one can guess that it doesn't embarrass me to pass on what little I've learned about how to work at achieving a measure of happiness. What I say may seem absurd to some, boring to others, but reading a book has at least one advantage over sitting in a classroom: one can quit the book at any time without seeming rude.

Taking a dull or unpleasant life (or day) and putting some brightness into it is something like making an ugly room attractive. The first job is to clean it and get rid of not only the dirt but also everything in it that displeases you. If the room is extremely dirty and if everything in it is distasteful to you and if you are short on time, energy, and money, you will have to do the thing gradually. Wash one window today, buy a small growing plant tomorrow, and train yourself, every time you go into the room, to see only the spot you have cleaned, the bit of brightness you have added, and think of the improvement you are planning to make tomorrow, not next year. By this method you will probably even enjoy that room long before you have it to your liking.

You can do the same thing with your undesirable life. In a way this is easier, for it takes no money, no physical energy, and no time which you must take from other activities. You need only patience and stick-to-it-iveness.

Let's say you are in a bad way; you worry, find fault, nag, are easily offended; you feel tense, overworked, put upon. As if that weren't unfortunate enough, you have a husband or wife who also nags, who has habits that annoy you, who argues at the drop of a hat, criticizes you and everyone else— well, I guess we've made it bad enough. Now how on earth can anyone in such a mess as that hope to get anywhere?

First, you must profoundly want a pleasanter life. Second, you can't be hazy about it. Third, you must realize that it will be a slow process and that you will have to work at it as you would at learning shorthand or golf. You will have to practice daily, hourly.

Think it over carefully and decide exactly what is making your life unharmonious. The pitfall in this analysis is that practically everything will turn out to be another person's fault, not yours, and let me warn you at once that you aren't going to get much of anywhere in this project by trying to change other people; you've got to change yourself.

If, in the following chapters, my suggestions sound almost childish—that is, if I ask you to treat yourself as you would a child—remember this: If you and a five-year-old were both starting to learn to play the piano, you would both have to begin at the bottom. *You* would have to learn the scales, too; you can't begin with sonatas just because you are grown up. And in this business of making a smooth life out of a muddled one, you are probably much worse off than a child would be, for you have had bad habits longer than he has.

We can pursue happiness with some hope of success if we stop expecting to find it in a star and look for it right here on earth. Happiness has been defined as inner peace and growth, and I like that definition, but it does seem to be a bit too vague to be of much help to anyone who is planning to take definite steps, tomorrow morning at the latest, toward building a happy life for himself.

Happiness is not in frequent bursts of exaltation but a simple, everyday state of being, and it must be reasonably stable, surely, if it is going to be of actual service to us. At any rate, that is the brand of happiness that I am going to try to get to the bottom of, and now I'll make an effort to frame a definition which suits this concept.

Happiness is a healthy, balanced enjoyment, which is steadily derived from the five senses, the mind, the emotions, and the spirit. In other words, it is taking the material we have to work with and using it to fill the hours of each day in a manner that will bring us a maximum of serenity and peace and a minimum of unpleasantness and pain and boredom. And when I speak of peace and serenity, I don't mean just peaceful surroundings or contentment. There must be an inner serenity which stays with us to a large extent, no matter what is going on around us. And peace, as I mean it, doesn't imply contentment with things as they are at any given time, but an inner calm no matter what is happening to us at any moment. Even this modest brand of happiness isn't achieved overnight, but it surely doesn't sound as frustrating as attempting to reach a star or trying to run without a stop from Maine to California. It is, at the very least, something that all of us can work toward and, little by little, certainly achieve to some degree. Every sunrise enjoyed, every troubled or unconstructive critical thought killed aborning, every serene hour lived through, brings its own small measure of inner peace and is one added stone in this castle of happiness we are building.

With this simple concept perhaps it isn't presumptuous or absurd for me to write about a few things that I have learned and many others I am trying to learn, in the hope that some of them may be of use to somebody. If anything I say will take the impatience out of just one man's voice, coax a smile into the eyes of only one woman, or encourage harmony in place of wrangling at some moment in one home, I shall not feel that I have wasted my time.

Besides, it won't stop there, for the softer voice, the smile, and the harmony will have their effect. If we could thoroughly grasp how far-reaching is the influence of our words and behavior, both for good and bad, we would probably think it quite worth while to open our hearts to the sun just for the sake of the general welfare, not even counting what it would do for us.

It may seem an odd jump, but I would like to mention my mother again, because she provides the best illustration I can think of in pointing out something that is absolutely basic if you're going to try to make your life happier.

Once a friend of mine said to me, "Do you realize that if your mother wasn't so thoroughly good, she would have been put either in an insane asylum or a jail long ago?"

I was startled, even though I knew she didn't mean it literally, but when she went on to explain what she had in mind, I agreed with her. For my mother did her own thinking and her own behaving. A birthright Quaker, she did what the spirit moved her to do, and if she was moved to do something, big or small, that all her world thought was completely cockeyed, she paid not the slightest attention and often didn't even know that anyone thought she was out of step. I never heard her try to justify herself to anybody, and she advised no one. "Thee listen to thy Inner Voice and I'll listen to mine" might have been her advice, if she ever stooped to give any.

Mother's nine children were grown before they realized how different she was from almost everybody else, and my guess is that she never did fully grasp it herself. In a way, she was detached; in a certain sense, I think she was incapable of giving credence to the motives behind many of the actions of other people. If, for instance, she had been asked why Mrs. A almost had a nervous breakdown worrying about the old worn rug in the living room (after all, it was only threadbare, not a hole in it), I'm sure Mother would not have answered that it was chiefly because Mrs. A couldn't bear what friends and neighbors must be thinking about it. If you had suggested such a notion to Mother, I think she would have been a little sorry for you, going about with such fantastic notions in your head.

How could there possibly be any reason for Mrs. A to want a new rug so badly except that she, herself, was sick of the old one? Why on earth should any of Mrs. A's friends care what kind of a rug she had, but if they did, wouldn't she be pleased and touched that they were fond enough of her to be interested in her home? As to that, it took me more than half of my lifetime to grasp the fact that people actually *do* care what the neighbors are thinking about the way they run their lives.

We might all become thinkers in our own right instead of robots if we were encouraged to use our brains or were just let alone when we were very young. Is it the fault of the parents that all too early the children stop asking "Why?" and begin to accept, conform, and go along with the herd? It would be fascinating to see a whole generation of human beings in which each individual had been allowed to think up his own rules of etiquette.

I don't at all mean that I'm in favor of children ruthlessly "expressing" themselves. They are going to live in a world where a little consideration for others is indicated now and then, and they will get a jolt somewhere along the line if they become too accustomed to running roughshod over others. There is a big gap between thoughtlessly doing as you please, no matter whom it hurts, and in using your head.

In recent years psychologists, social workers, college professors have had a good deal to say about teaching people to do their own thinking. I have even heard it said that one of the big advantages of going to college is that you learn to think for yourself. That seems to me as absurd as saying you go to college to learn to read. If by the time you enter college you haven't learned to do your own thinking, how on earth are you going to learn it there? Who is going to teach you? Do the professors know how to think for themselves? Can we teach something that we ourselves haven't learned?

Well, maybe we can if we want to badly enough. Perhaps it's simple; my mother was a genius at not interfering with her children's thinking, and that may be the whole secret. Since there were nine of us, the superficial answer might seem to be that she simply didn't have time to interfere. But of course that doesn't follow; the busier a mother is the more likely she is to lose patience and snap out orders and advice when everybody would be better off if she kept still.

As do all normal children, we quarreled and fought. If Mother happened on the field of battle (or perhaps she came deliberately, but if so she never let on), she suddenly remembered things she needed right away and sent us for them but in opposite directions. She never said that nice children don't hit each other (since nice children do and she never lied to us); she didn't tell us to stop fighting and she gave no indication that the errands were designed to stop or punish us. She was simply in a hurry for something.

But I remember one horrible time when she did punish one of my sisters and me; she made us kiss each other after a quarrel. We didn't let her catch us fighting for a long, long time after that. Did you ever kiss anyone you would have preferred to kick?

One of my brothers claims that she thumped him on the head more than once with her thimble when he wouldn't mind, but not hard enough to hurt. Her only other punishment was a veiled threat. If one of us got out of hand, she might say, "Run outside and see if you can find a nice little switch. It might come in handy if anybody should get naughty." It was somehow understood that we were to go out of doors and stay out for a while, but that we needn't bother about a switch. She never told us to bring one back—simply see if we could find one. Was it our fault that there wasn't a single switch to be found on a forty-acre farm?

Mother said, "No, you may not," or, "Don't do that," so rarely that, when she did, it held water. Once I remember she said no, it was too near suppertime, when two little neighbor girls asked us to go home with them. We told our friends the verdict, and they said, "Aw, go and coax her." We actually didn't know what they meant; the word "coax" we understood, but who on earth ever heard of coaxing a mother who had said no and had even given a sensible reason? No doubt it *was* too near suppertime.

We certainly never heard that peculiar query: What will people think? And as we grew into our teens there were, if possible, even less supervision and fewer comments. For instance, when I was about fifteen years old I attended some revival meetings and became rather overwhelmingly religious. I disapproved of pretty nearly everything, including the gambling we did (using matches for pennies), and among other reforms I kept hiding the playing cards from my brothers. But I didn't burn them, because I had relapses when I would bring out the cards and sit up half the night, playing pitch with the boys.

Mother made no remarks about either my fervor or my backsliding, and it never occurred to me to wonder what she thought about either. We both knew that I was following my Inner Voice, and probably both of us realized that it wasn't my fault that It couldn't make up Its mind.

I was just out of high school when I answered an advertisement for a young woman to go on the stage in a vaudeville act. It didn't say what the young woman was supposed to do, and since I could neither sing nor dance it seemed unlikely that I would qualify. Besides, vaudeville was beneath me; I was planning to be a great tragedian.

However, one must start somewhere so I answered the advertisement. The upshot was that I went on the stage with a man about thirty-five years old in a fake mind-reading act. The only remark my Quaker mother made was to my oldest sister, who was making the dress I was to wear in the act. Mother said, "I wouldn't make it very low in the neck if I were you."

I have a high opinion of my mother's tactics. True, none of us turned out to be perfect specimens; we had our quota of faults, neuroses, difficulties. There hasn't been a saint among us, and, judging by the number of times that God didn't pay any attention when I asked him to make me a good little girl, obviously He had other plans for me, and I suppose for the others, too. But we can thank both Mother and Dad that not one of us turned out to be a slave to convention; our thoughts, such as they are, are our own.

And so you will find my mother running through these pages, not only because she ordered her own life instead of letting it push her around, not only because she fits my modest definition of a happy person, but also, and perhaps most important, because she let the people around her alone, to follow their own destinies without interference or criticism from her. It is possible that it would have been better at times if she *had* interfered, but I am not claiming that she was perfect. It is happiness, not perfection, we're concerned about here, and they're not necessarily even related.

II

Humble Joys Are Better Than None

If one wants to get to the top of the ladder, the sensible procedure would be to start at the bottom and begin to climb. Let's pretend that we agree that our five senses provide us with the most elementary form of pleasure and start there in our search for happiness.

Some people are less richly endowed with sensitive taste buds than others, ranging from the "eat to live" school down to those who live to eat. Or should I say "up"? Which one is "superior" to the other, the man who swallows just any old thing because it's mealtime or the one who comes back from a vacation in Europe and can talk about nothing except the various splendid restaurants he visited? And make no mistake about it, these two men look down on each other.

Both extremes, I should think, are undesirable, and that was why I said "healthy, balanced" enjoyment in my definition, instead of merely enjoyment. The gourmet may have to do quite a lot of suffering to make up for his high order of gratification; he faces a possible catastrophe three times a day throughout his life. And the entire meal doesn't have to be inferior in order to upset him; just one item—an overdone roast or imperfect wine or weak coffee—will render his life hardly worth living. It's a feverish existence.

That is an extreme way of putting it, I know, but there are people like that. I know a man who suffers not only when he himself is faced with inferior food but also when he sees somebody else eating or drinking something that is below his standard. And it is amazing, but he can fill a whole evening with talk about food and drink if you let him. He's a nice fellow, but of course he's a bore, and the only thing to do when you have him to dinner is to ask a few other people as well, in the hope that, with their cooperation, he can be kept off his favorite (not to say only) subject. Why do I invite him? Because I like his wife very much and, in spite of his mania, I like him, too. Also, what a meal I get when I go to his house!

However, getting too much enjoyment out of a thing isn't a universal failing; getting too little is much more usual. As humble a pleasure as the sense of taste is probably worth enhancing, and I'm sure we can all cultivate our appreciation of flavors if we care to.

One way to do this is to pay real attention to what we are

eating and drinking. If, for instance, we read and eat at the same time and are getting any sense out of the book, can we be savoring our food? If time is of the essence and we are eating only to keep body and soul together, or if what we are eating is so unpalatable that it's wise to swallow it with our minds on something else, that is one thing. But since doctors say that most of us overeat, mightn't it be better just to read, and skip that meal entirely?

I'm quoting just about everybody when I say that at mealtime the atmosphere should be pleasant and the conversation light, but in these days of world tension you are pretty adept if you can manage this. In general, I am deficient in the art of guiding a conversation, but I remember how, during the Second World War, worry and depression took over to such an extent that sometimes I threatened my guests: I told them they couldn't have any dessert and I would give them instant coffee if they didn't change the subject. And they knew I meant it.

I don't think it's sensible for even generals to plan tomorrow's attack while they're eating, and it didn't seem reasonable to me for these relatively safe Americans to spoil their dinner (not to mention mine) by worrying about something they couldn't help, such as whether or not tomorrow's news would be worse than today's or how they would ever manage if the meat rationing didn't let up a little. It is true that I don't care for fruitless, gloomy talk even when I'm not eating, but at least one can think up errands in other parts of the house when dinner is over, particularly if one is the hostess.

Business lunches, which are so prevalent, don't seem wise

to me either. I don't think it's intelligent to try to work and eat at the same time, and if our minds aren't working while we talk business, what *is* happening? I have heard that ulcers abound among advertising men and also that much of their business is transacted at lunch. However, let's not jump to a hasty conclusion; probably just being in the advertising business is more than enough to give a man ulcers, but I see no point in making sure of it by adding the handicap of working while eating.

Although I'm in favor of adding to our pleasure by cultivating our taste, it doesn't seem worth while to learn to appreciate something that we probably won't be able to get hold of again for the rest of our lives. For instance, if you live in the city you're out of luck if you've learned to like vegetables only when they've come fresh from the patch. After thirty-two years of country living I have lost interest in vegetables which haven't just been picked or aren't my own fresh-frozen ones. Once you get used to raw tomato juice, as a special example, you can hardly get any other kind past your throat.

And if you aren't rich why learn to appreciate honest-to-goodness caviar? I had never eaten any when I went to Russia in 1923 to do famine relief work with the Quakers. My interpreter, a Russian prince, so handsome that it was hard to believe he hadn't just stepped out of a fairy tale, gave me a present of a quart of caviar (at least a thousand dollars' worth, I should think, in America). At first I didn't like it but I had to eat it, to avoid hurting his feelings, and unfortunately I learned to love it.

We are told that one way to enjoy food thoroughly is to stop smoking. I know a man who gave up cigarettes, and his wife has been in a dither ever since; nothing she cooks is quite up to the mark. That situation presents the negative side of the picture. Perhaps the next best thing to acquiring a worth-while experience is to avoid an undesirable one; therefore, if your wife can't provide savory food and there seems little likelihood that she will learn to, you could hardly do better than to cultivate an indifference to what you eat.

Years ago I came across something to the effect that the least tempting food becomes appetizing if you eat it with love. I didn't know precisely what that meant but, after all, why not try it? I found a piece of rather stale bread, which is an item I don't go for, especially without butter, and settled down to eat it but was a little confused as to what (or whom) I was supposed to love. Deciding that the idea was probably to love the bread, I ate it slowly, chewing it thoroughly and concentrating on how it tasted. It was surprisingly good.

You will draw your own conclusions about that; mine are something like this: Any experience, trivial or important, is likely to give us more pleasure if we are interested, unhurried, and are looking for the best the situation has to offer. It also helps if we *expect* something good, for in that case we don't overlook it if it's there in front of us. A stale piece of bread isn't the tastiest morsel in the world but neither is it loathsome. If as we eat it, we keep thinking how unfortunate it is that we haven't something decent, it won't be a treat, but if we are thinking nice friendly thoughts about it we might decide that it could be a whole lot worse.

There isn't any doubt that our thoughts about what we are

eating have a pretty strong effect. Have you heard about the baby (this is supposed to be true), who liked liver until one day his grandmother, who hated it, fed it to him? The child spat out the liver, apparently affected by the look of disgust on the grandmother's face. He didn't want any the next day either.

During the last war we fed guests over and over with rabbit, a food which they had said they couldn't stand. But we let them think it was chicken and, since they did like that, they ate the rabbit with pleasure.

I rather pride myself on eating everything; however, the glass of smoked grasshoppers which somebody gave me, and which I opened and tasted weeks ago, is, I notice, still in the refrigerator. I can't quite make up my mind to eat any more of them, yet how can I throw them out? I, who smile pityingly on people who shudder at brains and snake meat!

Mother's unexpressed attitude to food seemed to be that it was something neither to be scorned nor drooled over, but simply eaten or not, as one saw fit. There were always some appreciative remarks when we sat down to our favorite dish of navy beans simmered slowly with salt pork, but if we had carried on and on about how good it was, I feel sure that Mother would have quietly changed the subject without anyone suspecting that it was because she'd had enough of that topic.

We were never told that any particular item was good for us. Sweets weren't glorified by our being told that we must finish our vegetables before we could have any dessert. Anyway, I doubt if we always had dessert. We loved bread and molasses and sometimes filled our plates with more of it than we could eat, and although we weren't made to finish it at that meal it was put aside for us to eat later. This was not a punishment, but simply: "Here, this one belongs to you." Lucky! All fixed, with the molasses soaked well into the bread.

When, at an early age (I was about ten, I think), I decided to be ethereal as well as good, I cut down drastically on my eating. Sometimes I didn't even show up at mealtime; this struck me as a definite, practical short cut toward getting on top of that pedestal I had in view. In the diary I kept, at the end of each day's activities I'd write: "Ate one meal," "Ate two meals." I was ashamed of myself when I was obliged to write: "Ate three meals."

As far as I could tell, nobody paid any attention to my project. They didn't seem to miss me when I stayed away from the table, didn't notice how little I ate when I was there, and if any of them realized that I was getting ethereal by leaps and bounds, they didn't mention it. This must have gone on for about a year, and apparently it didn't hurt my health in any way. There was just one interlude: one of Mother's sisters came for a prolonged visit and, shocked, insisted that I be made to eat. Mother told her to take over; she did, I was made to eat more and, naturally, got a stomach-ache. After that they let me alone.

Later I was obliged to acquire an interest in food because when I got married I did the cooking, and to get just a passable meal onto the table one has to know what's passable. The upshot is that now I get more pleasure out of the sense of taste than I did formerly. I'm glad, for since I will spend some time each day for the rest of my life in eating, I can see nothing against enjoying it.

Just as we can eat food without tasting it, so we can hear sounds without being conscious of them. We get used to a ticking clock, a hissing radiator, city traffic, songs of birds, and don't even realize we're hearing them. And it is possible to live in the country year after year and never actually take in the gentle night sounds of various insects and other small animals —or is it fairies?

Brought up in Kansas by Quaker parents, and before the time of radio, record players, and so on, about the best in music I heard, until I was in my twenties, was the church choir or maybe *Hearts and Flowers* played on the piano. When we moved to New York we began at once to go to the Philharmonic and to the opera, not because we loved music but because we thought we might like it. We didn't want to miss anything this well-publicized city had to offer, from hansom cabs to symphonies.

At one of my first evenings at the opera I listened entranced to Caruso. Then, during intermission, my sister and I went to the ladies' room, where a very large woman was sitting on a small chair fanning herself and moaning almost hysterically because Caruso had done something he shouldn't have on some note or other. Mind you, he didn't go wrong on a whole aria, just one little note, and it looked as though that poor woman might not survive it. I, who had never heard Caruso before and had been in Heaven every minute he was on the stage, said to my sister, "Thank God I don't know *that* much about music!"

I have no real ear for music and never will know anything about it, and I am willing to believe I miss a good deal when I listen to it, but I doubt if I miss as much as those who are educated in it think I do. We're told that to get the most out of a symphony we should be able to follow the various motifs, and to recognize each instrument. I can do both of these things just well enough to realize that there is pleasure in them, to know that I'm missing something because I can't go the whole way. On the other hand, I can't seem to make myself care very much.

I took enough piano lessons to understand the pleasure one gets from following the score while somebody else is playing, but I remember that I had an uneasy feeling of antagonism when I first began to learn the notes. Until then I had responded to music as one does to the singing of a bird. Have you listened to the birds very early in the morning, beginning one after another to wake up and make sleepy sounds? These get louder, more and more birds enter in, and soon there's a whole orchestra. For me it would be quite a letdown to find that the birds had to learn all that, painstakingly, note by note. How tiresome if they had to follow rules! And if I tried to listen to them with education, so to speak, picking out this one and that one, as is done with the violin, the flute, the oboe, it would be a different kind of pleasure and for me a lesser one.

But since I'm all for getting the most out of everything we do, when I was told by people who "knew" music that one gets far more enjoyment out of it if one learns to recognize the various instruments, I set out to do just that. And it had its points; I could see what these people had in mind, but it didn't enthrall me. I still like to feel that music comes from an orchestra as it does from birds; I like to listen to it with my eyes closed and pretend that pixies are doing it, somehow, somewhere, and I don't care how or where. I'm sure I miss something but I can't help thinking the other kind of listener misses something else.

Some people like meat better than vegetables and vice versa. Some thrive on routine, others can't abide it, and so on, and the earlier we learn that our ways of behavior, our preferences, are not necessarily the best and certainly not the only ones, the better off we are. On the other hand, we don't have to be unduly humble and think they are the worst.

A few years ago I told a woman who had had an extensive musical education, and who knew that I was quite ignorant on the subject, that Brahms was my favorite composer. She was surprised; I asked her why and she said because Brahms is so difficult. I didn't know what she meant; his music was beautiful to me and what could be difficult about lovely sounds? I asked her but I don't remember what her answer was. In any case, I'm glad that nobody ever made me try to "understand" Brahms before I learned to love him; it might have spoiled everything.

I told this friend something that Deems Taylor once said, which had made me—and, I should think, all of the other ignoramuses—feel comfortable. He said not to wear yourself out trying to make music mean some definite thing. Once he was late to a concert, glanced at his program, listened a minute, and decided that this was the "babbling brook" movement. He settled himself comfortably and heard and enjoyed the babbling, and then discovered when it was over that that had not been the brook movement. Well! If Deems Taylor can be fooled, who am I to be ashamed?

I wish that people who have an ear for and an education in music didn't feel quite so superior about it, and I wish that those who haven't didn't feel apologetic. We can be grateful that we were born with a feeling for music, but I don't see how we can manage to be proud of it. It wasn't our doing. When, for instance, it comes to knowing Beethoven from Mozart, this can only result from familiarity with both of them. Even I can tell the difference, usually. It is like knowing maple from birch, if you handle wood, or a young broccoli plant from Brussels sprouts, if you grow vegetables. Is there something to feel uppish about in that?

It is of course true that the more sounds we learn to enjoy, the more we add to our pleasure in living. We can also let sounds drive us frantic: a dripping faucet, a ticking clock at night when we want to go to sleep, a neighbor's radio. For protection, it is wise to get over the annoyance these things cause us, if possible. I have a theory that usually we can get used to, and bear bravely, a noise that is completely impersonal, such as city traffic, but if it is a faucet that a husband should have fixed or a wife should have called the plumber about, a radio that a neighbor shouldn't play so loudly or so late—there's a long list. If our emotions enter in, we are lost indeed if we can't squelch them.

My guess is that noise is hard on us whether or not we are conscious of its bothering us. I believe that the quiet of the country is better for us than the noise of the city, although it is true that quiet in the country is now largely a thing of the past. What with airplanes, automobiles, farm machinery, lawn mowers, vacuum cleaners, radios and washing machines, country quietness is an anachronism. Some people even complain of the birds waking them early in the morning.

It is probably easier to learn to enjoy pleasant sounds than it is to manage not to mind the annoying ones. About all one has to do in order to cultivate an appreciation of enjoyable sounds is to remember to listen to them. As for the objectionable noises, we can try not to hear them and to some extent we will succeed. At least we can try not to resent them, not to be mad at the person responsible for them. Being annoyed will keep a person awake more effectively than benzedrine. If you need pepping up just think of someone you're furious with.

A voice too shrill, a laugh too sharp can just about spoil an evening for me. I've tried putting cotton in my ears, but someone is sure to ask me why and then I get involved, trying to think up a reason. Sometimes I've sat for an entire evening with a finger (unnoticeably, I hope) in the ear nearest the offender.

It may be that I am oversensitive to that kind of noise, but there is some compensation in the fact that I get a tremendous amount of pleasure out of listening to a beautiful speaking voice. I knew a man once, long ago, whom I think I would have married if he had asked me to, just because of his voice. If I could choose between a beautiful face and a beautiful speaking voice, I would by all means take the latter. I have to hear myself every time I say anything, but I can avoid looking in the mirror. And one's looks are likely to deteriorate while one's voice needn't.

Even for the sake of others I think I would make that choice. Unless I were repulsively ugly, people would get used to my appearance or they could to some extent avoid looking at me, but there is no way to avoid hearing a shrill and grating voice, and I think it gets on our nerves whether we realize it or not.

We can do a little something about our faces, but, I suspect, much more about our tone of voice. If we work at it we can learn not to talk too loudly, not to sound cranky, and even, I should think, to improve the timbre.

Am I getting off the subject of working toward happiness through our senses? I don't think so. When two or more people are together an atmosphere is created, and anything we can do to contribute to the over-all serenity and peace of the others involved will react to our benefit.

There have been tests, I believe, which show that many of us go about without seeing accurately what's going on around us. I am almost abnormal in this respect, or perhaps I should say subnormal. Apparently I look straight at people and things without seeing them. I met my father on the street once, glanced at him, and didn't realize who he was. And this has nothing to do with poor eyesight.

I never notice what a person is wearing unless it is, to me, very attractive or outstandingly ugly. This past weekend some friends stayed with us; the woman, who has plenty of money and, I wouldn't be surprised, better taste than I have, wore a dress so unbecoming that it all but spoiled my weekend. It actually pained me to look at her.

From this I would conclude that people who see with their conscious minds as well as their eyes must suffer more than I do, for there's quite a good deal of ugliness around. On the other hand, their eyes undoubtedly do more for their pleasure than mine do for mine. I don't get as much out of paintings and the like as I would if I didn't have this lack, and I know I miss many other lovely things.

In general, I consciously see only the very good or the very bad. I love cats and never miss noticing one, while I wouldn't even know a dog was around if he didn't invariably chew on my nylons. I've told my friends not to apologize to me if their houses need cleaning, for I certainly wouldn't know it if they didn't point it out to me.

Agreeable as it is to miss lots of ugliness, I think my condition is more to be pitied than envied for there is a great deal of beauty here and there which I miss. For instance, many years ago an artist called my attention to a bare tree against the sky in the middle of winter. I actually had never noticed that, but since then I really *see* bare branches against the sky every time I look at them and wonder how I ever could have missed them.

When I think of some thrills I have had by merely looking at something beautiful I realize that if I had cultivated the pure enjoyment of seeing, without any feeling attached, I would have added a good deal to my pleasure. I have always responded to the new moon, fluffy white clouds in a deep blue sky, the tender, yellowish green of spring, a bed of verbenas. However, these simple visual pleasures are not to be confused with the more complicated ones such as the Grand Canyon, a trusting catbird, the Russian steppe, which have meaning for me beyond the mere beauty.

My liking for a work of art (that is, painting, sculpture, and the like) seems to depend almost entirely on whether or not it has some significance. The smooth portraits of the elite cannot compare, for me, to those of workers, peasants, people who show some "living" behind the mere features. There was a painting in the Metropolitan Museum of Art (I suppose it is still there) of a young girl sitting in such a position that her knees are sort of high-lighted. A friend of mine would stand in front of that picture for a long time admiring those knees, which I would never have noticed if she hadn't called my attention to them. And they were worth noticing. On the other hand, there was a small statue in the Hermitage in Leningrad that I went back to look at again and again. It was of a beggar, an old man, and his face and even his posture showed cunning, tolerance, suffering, compassion, humor, cynicism. The point is that usually a thing has to have something beyond mere eye appeal in order for me to pay any attention to it. This is a deficiency.

My friend who appreciated those bare knees no doubt would have also enjoyed the statue, which means that she has a wider capacity for pleasure through her eyes than I have. This particular lack can be rectified; if I had taken the time to cultivate the capacity for observing, I would have got more out of my eyes through the years and might even have learned to appreciate modern art, although I'm not convinced that that would be an unmixed blessing.

The sense of smell and that of touch are somewhat different

from the other three. For one thing, people don't make a project of enjoying them as they do the others. It is possible that they aren't as easily developed as the other senses; I don't know of anyone who deliberately tries to.

We react readily to an offensive odor, even to the extent of becoming nauseated if it is strong enough. The smell of a skunk may make us sick, but many people actually like it if it is faint. And there are those who can't bear the heavy scent of tuberoses, which might delight them if it were more delicate.

If one cared to, one could easily develop an appreciation of fragrance. Just as in the cultivation of taste, sight, or hearing, this is largely a matter of paying attention. If you should see a lily in a vase, don't be satisfied with merely looking at it, smell it as well. If you buy a rosebush to plant, you can choose one whose blossoms have a fine fragrance. There are one or two white varieties which have the loveliest scent of any.

Do you know the smell of the warm earth, of freshly cut hay, of lilacs with the dew on them, of pine needles? If you live in the country, you can scarcely avoid the enchanting fragrance all around you, especially in the springtime. And yet, when friends come, it is a common thing to take them around the garden to see the beauty which abounds, but most unusual to conduct them on a smelling tour.

Enjoyment from touch is still lower in the scale; if you told someone you were trying to develop your sense of touch, I doubt if he would know what you meant. Yet we all have some feeling about it, such as disgust when we touch a clammy, slimy object. And many people who can look without discomfort at a dead rat caught in a trap might balk at picking it up with bare hands to dispose of it. Who cares to stroke a harmless snake? I happen to like to but here, of course, as with the dead rat, the thought about the animal is involved, not merely the feel of it. And I particularly like snakes.

Many women avoid wearing a woolen dress because it scratches, but few wear velvet primarily for the pleasure of touching it when their hands are lying in their laps. Almost everyone appreciates the feeling of wood, yet if metal furniture comes into style it doesn't seem to occur to most people that wood is much pleasanter to rest one's arms on.

Of all the senses, that of touch is the most widely ignored for aesthetic pleasure, but it stands first if you connect it with emotion. To look at the face or listen to the voice of someone we love cannot compare with touching his hand or holding him in our arms. If a child is hurt, if a friend is unhappy, the natural and comforting thing is to put our arms around him. To *touch* him.

The five senses have this in common: they are fleeting and diminish from minute to minute. The first taste of anything is by far the best; if all of a Daiquiri tasted as good as the first sip I might become an addict. I have heard that gourmets claim that cocktails spoil the sensitivity of taste. I believe that the first sip or bite of anything begins to lessen the appreciation of it, so a poor cook could do worse than to serve delicious canapés and not worry about the meal itself.

The same is true of seeing. Whether it is a painting, a flower bed, or a bird or a beautiful child, one can't keep alive the first few moments of delight. Scenery along the road will

begin to pall after a while, even though it is constantly changing as one goes along. The first mile is the best. Have you
ever been driving with somebody in the spring when all the
foliage is new and lovely, or in the fall when everything is
running riot, and been forced to listen to his continual ex-
clamations and his demands that you look, and look again?
Haven't you been tempted to say to your companion, "Enough
already"?

I'm sure I would have learned to appreciate and like painting and sculpture more than I do if visiting art museums
hadn't been the means by which I tried to cultivate my taste.
There is so *much* to see and to make the trip for only three or
four pictures, then go again to look at a few more never seemed
worth the effort. A flower garden crowded with many kinds of
flowers has little appeal for me, nor has a room overcrowded
with beautiful antiques or beautiful anything. Even an isolated
bed of *Phlox drummondi* or of verbena, so startlingly beautiful when one first glimpses them, cannot hold my attention
for very long. Soon I wander away and look at other things;
when I come back, the phlox and verbena will enthrall me
again.

It is for this reason that I greatly prefer to have as many
things as possible be useful as well as beautiful. Recently a
friend showed me a rather oddly shaped piece of wood which
she had just bought.

"What is it for?" I wanted to know.

"Does it have to be *for* something?" her husband asked.
"Can't a person just hang it on the wall and look at it?"

"But you'll soon get so used to it that you won't even see it,"

I objected. "Whereas if you use it for something, it sort of comes and goes in your scheme of living, and each time you use it you'll really see it and admire it all over again."

There is no doubt that this is true. On the wall by the couch where I spend my reading and resting hours is a lovely Chinese painting, but I'm so used to it that I enjoy it only when somebody mentions it. On the other hand, the delicate coffee cup I use and wash and put away and take out and use again is an ever-recurring pleasure.

Music can hold our attention longer because it is constantly changing, but just let the record of your favorite symphony get stuck at your best-loved passage and see how long you can stand it. Or let a bird go on and on; once my sister stepped to the door and said to a whippoorwill singing lustily in a nearby tree, "Please, *please!* You've said that often enough."

If a sound, however enthralling, keeps repeating itself, after a while you either don't hear it at all or it gets on your nerves. A waterfall, the hum of insects, the redwing's call can take you right up into the clouds, but you won't stay there long. Ecstasy and lofty inspiration and poignant thrills are short-lived.

Fragrance is even more fleeting and elusive. The scent of the large gardenia plant in our living room charms everyone who comes in when it is covered with blossoms, but I am so used to its fragrance that I must go up to it and sniff a blossom in order to appreciate it. I'm fond of perfume but it seems a waste to put it behind my ears; instead, I put it on my wrists and on a handkerchief and every now and then inhale the fragrance. When sweet peas and lilies of the valley are in season my sister keeps a vase of fresh ones on the table near the couch where I read; often, through the evening, I lean over and smell them, but the interlude is essential. I couldn't stay conscious of the scent for long at a time.

One of the pleasantest, most relaxing physical sensations I know is any one of the various forms of massage. I go through the three or four hours of getting a permanent with pleasure, because of that relatively short time when the operator is massaging my scalp. When we were children we ran our fingers lightly up and down each other's forearms. "I'll trade you ten," or "I'll trade you twenty," we would offer. But the person who does it must know how. Merely to keep rubbing in the same spot even if ever so lightly, is no good at all. And it mustn't go on too long; only a glutton would want to trade fifty.

The main thing is to be alert, to remember to pay attention. How much pleasure can you get out of an apple? If it is handsome, either in shape or color, you can enjoy it through your eyes. Next you can smell it, then feel how smooth it is. Now as you bite into it, listen, and you may hear a pleasant crackle; we learned to enjoy that sound when we were youngsters. And as you eat it you will savor the taste.

For the height of aesthetic pleasure I might choose a white single peony. I know of nothing which is lovelier to look at and I know of no finer, more delicate fragrance. And the large satiny petals simply beg you to touch them; they look so fragile, yet you can smooth them gently with your fingers and do them no harm.

Now do I hear some impatient grumbling? Is someone saying, "Well, if eating an apple and smelling a flower is what she calls happiness, I guess we can all be happy. She could have saved herself the trouble of writing a book."

Well, of course, that's not all there is to it, but let's agree that we've gone a step farther than gulping down food without tasting it and looking at a flower without smelling it. We started at the bottom of the ladder, remember? If our three-year-old boy tells us he wants to learn trigonometry, we first must teach him how to add one and one. Unless you have progressed farther than the majority have in learning how to be happy, you will do better to start at the beginning. Yes, I know that many of us are searching for something lofty, something fine and almost beyond description, but I doubt if we will find it if we can't even keep enough of our attention on the food we are eating and on the scents and sounds and sights around us to get a reasonable share of the pleasure they have to offer.

By all means let us often look up at the stars as we walk through life, but if, now and then, we don't glance down at the path we are traveling, I am afraid we will have just one tumble after another.

III

Making Our Minds Toe the Mark

There are probably quite a large number of people who wouldn't agree with me about some of the best ways to enjoy our minds. For instance, I don't think that cramming them full of information that we will probably never make use of rates very high, although that may be because most of the facts I accumulate have a way of trickling through and disappearing into space—that is, those which don't interest me while I'm acquiring them.

A long time ago one of Mother's sisters came from Ohio to Kansas to visit us, and one day she asked Mother how far it was to such and such a place.

"I don't know," Mother said. "We'll ask John when he comes home." (John was my father.)

My aunt replied, "You say that all the time. You won't know anything if John dies first."

Mother laughed and said, "I don't know much, it's true, but at least I know where to go to find out things. If John dies first, I'll have to hunt up another source of information."

I know other people besides Dad who carry great quantities of facts around in their heads and always seem to have room for more. As far as I can tell, they get a good deal of pleasure out of this brand of hoarding; they have inquisitive minds and one can see the fun they're getting when they run into some new piece of information. There is an eager, interested expression on their faces and often it doesn't seem to make much difference what the new subject is.

That is one way to enjoy our minds and one that will never fail us, I should think, since there is an inexhaustible supply of things waiting to be investigated, but it doesn't happen to be my way and I have never had the slightest urge to try to adopt it.

However, I can be just as inconsistent as anybody, and here is a story to prove it. When I was thirteen years old, attending a small school in the country, I thought that studying geography was a great waste of my valuable time; who could possibly manage to care what city was capital of which state or where a river started and where it stopped? So inside the big flat geography I had a fascinating book about villains abducting heroines, and heroes coming to the rescue, and I read that instead of the geography lesson, trusting the teacher to show reasonable tolerance when I couldn't tell him which gulf was where.

I assumed that the teacher was paying a compliment to my superior mind when he asked me to take over the fourth grade geography class and have them recite their lessons to me, but I realized some time later that he was desperate and hoped that I might learn something that way. I was delighted with the project and I recall vividly my surprise and disgust when I asked a child some question he couldn't answer. There it was right there in the book, for pity's sake; how could anyone with any brains at all fail to see it and to remember that Augusta is the capital of Maine and is on the Kennebec River? (*If* I'm right!)

After a while I saw the absurdity of my double standard and reformed to the extent of improving on my daily recitations, but I didn't care enough about geography to remember what I learned. To fortify my ignorance I think I worked up some kind of snobbishness about it, and I still feel a little like apologizing for remembering about Maine and Augusta but at least I have a good excuse: somebody made up a song about the capitals of the states, and it started with Maine, so I remember that one.

Reading is, to some extent, a passive way of enjoyment through the mind, but even so what a boon it is for those who like it! In our family of nine children there was one sister who didn't read much until later in life and a brother, Walt, who read very little. The rest of us were greedy readers.

As we were growing up my father interfered with us almost as infrequently as my mother did, but, getting so much out of reading himself, he couldn't believe that anyone else wouldn't, once he got into it. So Dad made a rule that if Walt wanted to go out after supper he must first read for half an hour. Walt obeyed, or at least he sat down and looked at a book, when he wasn't glancing at the clock. But it didn't take; on his eighteenth birthday he announced, "I'm a man now and can do as I please and I'm not going to read unless I want to."

There was one kind of reading, though, which he thoroughly enjoyed. My oldest brother, Bob, liked to get hold of some melodramatic novel and read it aloud to us younger ones, and not for anything would Walt have missed that performance. He watched our expressive faces and grinned with delight as we gasped over the near-successes of the villain and sighed over the hard luck of the heroine.

From this one instance it would be absurd to jump to the conclusion that a person who doesn't naturally like to read can't learn to care for it. (As a matter of fact, Walt did read quite a lot, later on.) The sales of paperbacks these days indicate that a lot of people are reading books who never did so before, and even a bad book may have its purpose, for the reader is likely to try another—and better—one.

Why should anyone learn to enjoy reading? Leaving out such reasons as broadening our minds, getting other people's points of view, gathering knowledge and information, and pure enjoyment, love of reading has a few definite, practical advantages. All you need is reasonably good eyesight and the ability to get to a library, or someone who will go for you. The cost is almost nothing. Unlike physical activities, no strength is required. You need only to be able to hold a book and, if it is a heavy one, prop it up on a pillow. I mean that last seriously; if relaxation is as beneficial as I believe it is, it is a mistake not to be comfortable while you are reading.

There are other advantages: a book won't get out of order, as the radio or television may; unless the house burns down, it won't desert you; if a thief breaks in, it is about the last thing he will take away with him. By dying, or moving away, or merely getting fed up with you, your family and friends may forsake you, but you can read when completely alone. With a stirring novel you can temporarily forget your troubles; some books might even start you to thinking, presenting you with another fascinating pastime.

So much for reading. What about conversation? It is prevalent enough; in fact, just try to avoid it. What do we get out of it? Not much more than we put into it, I imagine.

I don't know whether or not anybody knows precisely what he means when he talks about "the lost art of conversation." I, for one, am not sure whether it is something to regret having lost, or not. Broadly speaking, I haven't much admiration for our present brand, but maybe I should have. Let's have a look at it. For our model we'll use a group of six people gathered together for dinner. Two of them would like to talk politics; another one, cooking and recipes; a fourth has a choice bit of gossip he's dying to go into at some length; a fifth (it is spring) can think of nothing but his garden; and the sixth has just sold his first water color and can hardly wait to steer the conversation to painting so that he can slip in his exciting news. But any one of these subjects is going to leave a few people bored.

I suppose this intricate situation is what gave birth to "small talk," although I have never been clear as to exactly what that expression means. If some child asked me to define it, I might tell him it was like a conversation in which each person spoke a different language and nobody understood any language but his own, but it wouldn't matter because nobody would miss anything worth hearing.

I believe in thinking of ourselves first in our attempt to enjoy life, and each time I say this someone is shocked at such a selfish attitude, so once more I have to point out that we think of ourselves first when we buy a car, new clothes, take a trip, go to the beauty parlor and why is it more selfish to consider ourselves first when we search for happiness than when we go looking for a few new records? Or go to an expensive restaurant or to a play? In no case do I mean we should enjoy ourselves at the expense of others, and now at this dinner party we're in a predicament. We want to talk about music, for instance, but nobody else does. It boils down to a question of boring or being bored, or searching for a topic that will appeal to everybody.

I think there is a way out, although I have never had the enterprise or skill to try it more than a few times. Those times it worked. Almost always, in even a small gathering, a definite, specialized subject is likely to leave at least one or two people out of things. But I do think that almost everybody has an interest in, and perhaps an opinion on, many general subjects.

The first time I tried out this theory it was with no intention of experimenting, and actually I did it when it was unnecessary. Fred and I were having dinner with our nieces and nephews—Virginia, Roger, Millard, and Gerry—and we all were interested enough in each other not to need any "art" in the conversation. However, I had recently been pondering two or three questions and was curious about what answers I would get on them from people in general. So I proposed one:

"I know a woman who complains that certain of her guests follow her from stove to sink to table when she is trying to get a meal ready, and they talk constantly. But she, too, does this and, hard as it may be to believe, she has told me about her friends doing it while I am in the process of getting dinner onto the table. How can an imaginative and intelligent person (which she is) possibly do that?"

A lively discussion followed; everyone had an opinion. When that subject was exhausted, I submitted: "I believe it is a known fact that men die younger than women; could this be because men, even boys, aren't supposed to cry, and psychologists now tell us that it's bad for us to hold in our emotions?"

They went to bat on that one. When I had exhausted my meager supply, Virginia said, "This is such fun. Haven't you any more?"

I hadn't at the moment, but the others began to contribute; there is no end to that sort of topic. And the group doesn't have to be cultured, intellectual, informed. That is the beauty of an abstract, or a general subject. Everyone, from the person who never got through the eighth grade to the college graduate, has an opinion on whether or not there is free will, whether boys are harder to raise than girls, whether inheritance is more important than environment. And the contributions of those of small education are often the most interesting, because they aren't simply a rehash of things they have learned from study, repeated parrot-like.

The person who is a genius in his ability always to talk about what you are interested in is an asset when you are alone with him, but in a group he can't be of much help. And even when it is just between you two, you get onto him in time and realize that he isn't pining to hear you go on and on about *your* pet subject. This eventually cramps your style; even the most egotistical of us prefers that our audience enjoy us when we hold forth.

I am always slightly embarrassed when a finishing-school product performs; I have never come across one so skillful that I couldn't sort of feel the rules of the textbook hovering in the background. When it comes right down to it, I doubt if there could be anyone so expert in conversation that one couldn't hear the machinery creaking if it is actually a studied performance, and perhaps that was my unconscious reason for not further pursuing my idea of introducing general topics; inevitably I would run out of material and be obliged to use the same things over and over. It would then deteriorate into a stunt, seem forced, and lose any charm it might have when spontaneous.

However, I am not as pessimistic about all this as I may sound, or perhaps I should say that, as far as I am personally concerned, I manage to make out reasonably well and practically always have a good time at dinner parties. If I'm a guest I can usually manage to be near someone I like to talk with, at least before and after the meal, and, as hostess, well, since

I invite people to my home not to do them a favor but because I want to see them, there is surely something wrong with me if I don't manage to get pleasure out of it.

As for my guests, if someone is obviously having a thin time of it, I try to do something about it, but I have no good word to say for the woman who *works* at being a hostess. You can spot this, however adept she may be, and when she goes so far as arbitrarily to order her guests to change seats and talk to someone else, it becomes a performance rather than a party.

Meditation (contemplation) is rated highly among those who practice it. The Quakers "go into the silence"; the yogis go far in this field. If you have never been to a Quaker meeting, the kind where there is no minister, I wish you would do it sometime and see how you like it. For me it is a most restful experience. Everyone sits in silence, but if somebody feels like getting up and reciting a poem, a bit of philosophy he has read, a favorite verse from the Bible, or some thought of his own, he does so.

The art of contemplation appeals to me, but I don't practice it; I find it impossible to lose myself in meditation if I have a deadline. If it is four o'clock and I know that at six I have to go and start dinner, I simply can't lose myself in anything even remotely resembling "high" thoughts. So I don't try.

Once, about twenty-eight years ago, I felt quite strongly that I wanted to do a worth-while job of meditating. On our place, up a hill, we had a small hut, one room, with no water, no stove—just an army cot, a chair, and a table. I sometimes went there for a few hours to be alone, to read or to write. This time I planned to go up there and stay for three days and nights. It was in September; I had worked hard in the garden all summer besides doing the housekeeping and feeding untold guests, and I was tired out and had a cold. I set out on a Sunday evening. A friend (a physician), who had spent the weekend with us, tried to persuade me not to go until my cold was better, but I didn't want to put it off.

So after dinner I went, taking a good-sized basket of tomatoes from our garden for food and drink. I went to bed at once on the not-very-comfortable army cot and, being even tireder than I realized, slept all night, all through the next day, and well into the following night.

When I finally became fully aroused there was a most interesting, if unappealing, development: I was in a rage and after all this time I'm not quite clear about it. But I think I was furious about things that had happened far back, not in childhood, but not in recent years either. I don't know how long my anger lasted, but I think not more than an hour. Then, quite suddenly, it evaporated.

I got up as soon as it was light. There were two days left for the meditating, and I didn't attempt it in any definite or methodical way. I spent those two days mostly sitting in the rather comfortable chair, neither reading nor writing, of course, and I didn't go out of doors where there would have been all sorts of distractions. I had nothing to eat or drink but tomatoes; my cold disappeared.

I'm vague about the results; they weren't startling and not even very conclusive. As I remember, I had some worthy, constructive thoughts, maybe even a few lofty ones, and I hope that to some degree they have stood by me.

I was glad when the time was up, but I have a pronounced feeling that I would get something valuable out of it, in the way of relaxation and inner peace, if I could do this for twenty-four hours once a week. I would like to very much, but the hut is no longer there.

Fred used to say that he thought I could meditate here in the house. Perhaps some people could, but I knew it wouldn't work for me. I could have gone through the motions perhaps, but what with the telephone and all other interruptions and activities, which, strangely enough, are more frequent in the country than in the city, I could never have kept my mind on it sufficiently to get anywhere. Fred said that he would see to it that I wasn't disturbed, but there is no place in this two-hundred-year-old house that is safe from the various noises around. Since it was my job to cope with milkman, laundry, telephone, and so on, it would have been difficult, if not impossible, for me to empty my mind of all this for an entire day. One small item: Fred always hated answering the telephone but he couldn't let it ring, unanswered, so that every time I heard it I would have been pulled out of the clouds and would have begun to pity Fred. And neither could he get his own meals with any pleasure.

Now that he is gone and I live alone with no one depending on me, perhaps I could lock the door, ignore telephone and callers, fast for one day, and let thoughts come and go and refresh my spirit. I would like to try it; the drawback is there are so many other things I like to do. If you want to go to

Mexico and to Russia, you can't do both on the same week-end.

I have never been on a train or in a beauty parlor when the large majority of the people weren't reading. In fact, all women do in the beauty parlor; the girls still offer me a magazine, although I've been going to the same place for almost thirty years and have never yet accepted the offer. I suppose this means that few people set out just to think. If you aren't sick but lie in bed after you wake up, nobody assumes that perhaps you are thinking; you're merely lazy. And who ever sits down to think, as one does to read?

I don't pretend to be any good at original, constructive thinking, any more than I am at meditating, but I can see that it might be a fascinating occupation. For one thing, you can rest your overworked eyes while you do it. For another, your thoughts have a chance of being your own while what you read is secondhand. I welcome other people's clothes, but I don't feel so hospitable about others' thoughts. I'm delighted to consider them, but adopting them is something else.

Mother's culture was in the realm of thought. She read a good deal, but not ravenously. During the years we spent in New York there was no new idea, no religion, that she didn't investigate. No lecture was too radical, none too reactionary —for that matter, none too absurd. When we teased her about it she would say, "There's a little good in everything; I take the good and leave the bad."

Doctors and laymen, as well as psychologists and Christian Scientists, are learning rapidly that the mind controls the body to a startling degree. I know it from my own experience. From the point of view of our physical health, it is important to have healthy thoughts and an ability to relax. And it's important for our happiness, too, for although we don't have to be healthy in order to be happy, it helps considerably.

There is one thing about our thoughts, however, that is obvious, and yet we don't take nearly as much advantage of it as we might. Life is full to the brim with desirable and undesirable things that are beyond our control. Few of us have as much money as we would like to have; most of us can't do with our time the things that we wish we could. The wrong people show up unexpectedly while the right ones get caught in a blizzard and can't make it; the baby cries when it isn't necessary, the dog won't mind, the car won't start, the tomatoes won't grow, the milkman is late—you could go on forever.

But just about the most important thing in your life, for your own serenity, you can control, once you make up your mind to do it. You can guide your own thinking and, through that to a large extent, your emotions, and surely it is what we are thinking and feeling that brings us happiness or unhappiness.

It is nothing short of wonderful to know that we have a choice. We can stew over Mrs. A, who gets us down, but we don't have to. What's wrong with thinking about Mrs. B, who is such fun and is understanding and considerate? We can think with great annoyance about our wife's bad habit of always being late, but what for? It won't help at all, and it's just as easy to think about her attractive smile.

There is no end to the disagreeable thoughts we can mull over if we are foolish enough to do it, but there is also no end to the good ones; the great good luck is that we have a choice. We may not be able to choose between this expensive perfume and that cheaper one, perhaps we can't have the car we want, we may not even be able to have the husband or the cut of meat we'd prefer, but thoughts are free, available to us all.

There's another comforting thing. The person you want to see and talk to may drop in and delight you, then along may come somebody who has already said everything you care to hear and spoils your pleasure, but not so with thoughts. Once you let in a welcome one and *keep* it there safe in your mind, no undesirable one can push its way in. There isn't room there for two thoughts at a time. And if the bad one does edge its way in, you can throw it out as you cannot bring yourself to do with an unwelcome guest.

If you have let yourself get into the habit of entertaining the kinds of thoughts that make you go about with a tense or critical or dissatisfied or depressed look on your face, you cannot overnight begin entertaining only desirable guests in your mind. It is going to take some practice to push the bad ones out and let the good ones in, but don't be discouraged if at first it is uphill work. Every minute that you consciously, deliberately spend in constructive rather than destructive thinking is so much to the good. Practice a little on seemingly insignificant things. If you gave a dinner party and the guests arrived late, the roast beef was overdone, the peas flat, the potatoes watery, the pie crust tough, think of the dill pickles. They were awfully good, somebody said.

IV

Growing Up Emotionally

If we want to badly enough, and make a determined effort, we can cultivate the five senses and control our thinking, but how are we going to go about acquiring desirable emotions? I may get into hot water here, may decide I am drawing incorrect conclusions while I'm in the middle of a sentence and be obliged to cross it out and start over, but I'm going to try.

If a child made up a list of things that cause unhappiness, it might go like this: a sore throat, when Mother scolds, the dentist, I shouldn't have told a fib, always have to finish my milk, the puppy dies, Mother and Daddy have a quarrel, afraid Sister will tell on me, not getting a bicycle for Christmas, the kids might make fun of me. A grown person's list would, up to a point, be similar, although expressed in different terms: sickness, disapproval, death of a loved one, anger, fear, guilt, physical pain, being forced to do things we don't like to do, ridicule, wanting things we can't afford.

Actually, however, if the adult would think further, he would have to add some items that wouldn't appear on a child's list, and these would, oddly enough, be trifles: the dinner party wasn't a success, the secretary came in a half-hour late, Jim beat me at golf again, Laura's new coat is prettier than mine, and so on. Our days are full to running over with annoyances that have no importance until we magnify them and permit them to spoil an hour for us—time which we could fill with something pleasant, or at least unobnoxious.

I said something like this in another book I wrote, and yesterday I received a letter from a young woman who had just read it. She said, in part: "For so long I have lived with a nagging sense of guilt about the way I keep house and find time for myself. No longer! We live in a rural neighborhood of other young families, and I have sensed a sniffing superiority from other mothers as to my methods of housecleaning, child-raising, and freedom to 'do.' Since reading your book I don't push it at the 'girls,' but I sure wave it like a flag. Thank you for making my step lighter, my way clearer, and, above all, my time not stolen but earned."

But when we try to decide what emotions bring unhappiness (with, I hope, the intention of getting rid of them), we will find that not all of them are connected with other people.

There are other kinds of fear besides that of being criticized: fear of not getting along materially, of sickness, of death, of falling below our standards in our own estimation. Then there is that nameless fear—the feeling of impending doom—which some people are cursed with. I suppose the last is a form of sickness, and I am certainly not equipped to tell anyone how to cope with it, but it seems to me that we can do a little something about the others.

For the first two, isn't it simply a matter of thinking constructively rather than destructively, keeping our minds on prosperity and health rather than their opposites? Or perhaps we could use a little imagination and discover how piddling it is to pick out only a few things to be afraid of; while we're about it, why not make a good job of it? We know that disaster can descend upon us at any moment. How dare we get into a bathtub, for instance, and maybe slip and break a leg? Or get in a car, or even just walk along the sidewalk? Nor can we stay "safely" at home; household accidents abound. How dare we eat in a restaurant? Every now and then we hear of food poisoning. And even if everybody seems to love us, mightn't we be murdered? Read mystery novels, and you will find that often the corpse had (as far as he knew) no enemies. If we are afraid of anything at all, why be choosy, why not just be afraid of everything, have a good laugh at ourselves, and relax?

I don't understand how anyone can manage to be afraid of death, whether he believes in a God or not. As for me, I would have to believe in One who is not only merciful but also just, and if He is, He wouldn't put me here with faults and weaknesses, then, when I die, punish me because I wasn't perfect. On the other hand, if I don't believe in immortality, all my troubles will be over when I die; it will be like going to sleep without having to worry about what is going to happen tomorrow.

The fear of falling below our own standards is first cousin to a feeling of guilt, and I don't understand that feeling either. I have done many things I shouldn't have, and have failed to do others, and am sorry, but unless I am extremely conceited I must admit that, like everyone else, I'm not perfect, and never will be. I will make an attempt to improve, but to go around feeling guilty will help no one, so I will skip it.

To get back to making a list of the things that cause unhappiness, few of us would include a cold in the head, but we would all agree on the serious illness of someone we care for. Once when I had a head cold and was making rather a to-do about it, I flippantly remarked that if I had a fatal disease I could be as brave as the next one, but who was going to admire me for being stoical about a common cold? For that matter, who was even going to notice that I had one and condole with me, if I didn't carry on about it?

It is almost routine to come through with flying colors in times of great stress; our best qualities seem to rush to the rescue while serious trouble lasts, then they take a much-needed rest between calamities. People become oblivious to the daily annoyances when a member of their family lies at death's door, but just let the loved one get through the door on the desired side and begin to convalesce, and everyone, including the patient, starts right in again to overreact to every trifle.

For people to snap at each other and get upset over nothing after a spell of worry and strain isn't surprising; it does seem strange, though, that, having just lived through an enormous trouble, we don't automatically take it casually when, say, the applesauce boils up all over the clean stove.

Of course, behaving commendably through a period of serious trouble isn't actually automatic, and if someone should ask me how to learn to do it, I wouldn't have the faintest idea what to tell him. The surprising amount of emotional steadiness which shows up, seemingly from nowhere, in times of stress appears to me to be analogous to the second wind which comes to our aid when we need extra physical strength for an emergency. I'm sure I wouldn't know how to go about laying in a supply of either emotional stamina or second wind for a rainy day.

Disliking the people around us is another thing we might add to our list. Assuming that it gives us more pleasure to like someone than to dislike him, how are we going to accomplish this? Let's start off by admitting that no matter what we do, or how hard we try, we aren't going to like everybody, let alone love them. We are, after all, creatures with some taste and discrimination, and we don't care for all music, all colors, all books, all pictures, all odors—how could we be expected to like all people? True, the more of them we manage to take a fancy to, the pleasanter our lives will be, and we are simply lucky, not praiseworthy, if we can find something that appeals to us in the large majority of persons we see frequently.

I am not talking now of approval and disapproval; criticism of others will come in a later chapter. Recognition of a person's good qualities doesn't make us like him, and to a large extent we are helpless in our feelings about people; we can perhaps cultivate a taste for olives if we keep on eating them, but this seems to work just the other way in our taste for people; the more we see of someone we couldn't stand in the first place, the harder he is, usually, for us to take as time goes on.

So what can we do? If we should happen to have an aversion to any of the people we see now and then and only briefly, such as a milkman or grocery clerk, we just ignore it and charge it up to profit and loss. For many years we had the same milkman, and just the sight of his wagon made me feel good. On the other hand, simply to pass the house of a person who rubs me the wrong way makes me vaguely uncomfortable. But I don't have to dwell on my antipathy.

A business relationship should be easy to handle, as a rule. If you don't like your boss, look for another job; if you don't like your secretary, fire her. And that last isn't as heartless as it sounds, for I can think of few things which would be harder on me than spending the greater part of my waking hours with someone I disliked or who disliked me. So, if your secretary hasn't the initiative to resign, do her a big favor and discharge her. If I were doing it, I would probably tell her why. "Look here, your work is all right but you and I don't hit it off. We're bad for each other; I'll give you a month to find another job." Then hope to goodness you'll like the next secretary.

I believe it is scarcely possible to exaggerate the harm it can do, or at least the extent of discomfort it causes, to be with people to whom we have an aversion. It is undesirable enough to live with pictures we dislike, colors which repel us, a radio going if it isn't our doing; it is much worse to spend time with people who are hard on us.

I knew a family who had two boys, one two years old, the other five. The older child violently hated their nurse; he couldn't bear to have her touch him, and his whole character seemed to change when she came into the room. Now, I can write whole books telling people what to do and what not to do, since they can't argue back except by letter, but I am diffident about telling any individual how to behave. However, I did tell the mother of this child what I thought about her keeping that nurse who, incidentally, seemed innocuous enough to me.

The mother answered, "I couldn't possibly let her go; she's wonderful with the baby. I know Johnnie can't bear her, but she's not doing him any harm. Actually, she's the one I'm sorry for; he's so rude and disagreeable to her."

Of course I dropped the subject. If a mother can't see for herself that it isn't fair to a child to saddle him day after day with a person who brings out the worst in him, what could I say to convince her?

Let's take a fleeting glance at married couples who would like to get a divorce but decide to stay together for the sake of the children. Even when husband and wife love each other, there is bound to be a certain amount of bickering, irritability, quarreling to which the youngsters are subjected, but I believe most children are sensitive to the difference between arguments and tension with love in the background, and without it.

Once a little girl whose parents are stoically staying together for her sake spent a few days with us, and she said to me wistfully, "Don't you and Fred have fights? My father and mother have lots of fights."

I told her that by the time two people had lived together for thirty years, and were as old as Fred and I were, they had done just about all of their fighting and that her father and mother would get over it.

She answered in a worried tone, "I don't think they'll ever stop because I don't think they like each other very much."

She was right; they didn't. And she was only six years old.

To some extent one can follow the reasoning of these mothers and fathers and at least give them a high mark for good intentions. But what motivates those people, usually relatives, who have no strong practical reason for living together but who do it automatically, so to speak, and yet constantly get on each other's nerves?

I am thinking of two sisters I used to know. They were widows, had independent incomes, and they shared an apartment. Each disapproved strongly and volubly of what the other ate, wore, read, right on up and down the line. Criticism and quarrels were rampant. Not once, apparently, did it occur to either one of them that they could live in separate apartments, see each other when they chose, and perhaps, then, even enjoy each other.

The best way I know of for smothering my aversion to someone is to feel sorry for him, and unfortunately there is hardly a person who doesn't rate compassion for one reason or another. If nothing better offers, you can pity him because he doesn't appeal to you; he probably guesses that he doesn't and would be more comfortable if he did.

Many of our other undesirable emotions can be lessened or done away with entirely with conscious endeavor, and, since we are making this attempt in order to find happiness for ourselves, I will remind you once again that this has nothing to do with hiding our dislikes, irritability, anxiety. We must, of course, learn not even to feel these emotions if we are to achieve serenity.

Now psychologists are telling us not to hold back our feelings; if we feel like crying, or screaming, or whatever, go ahead and do it. I don't know how long we are supposed to keep up this performance before we are cured, if ever, and I don't know enough about it to dare say I am against it (and I'm not at all sure that I am), but I should think it would be rather hard on the people we live with. And if the whole family felt like letting go at once, it could get pretty noisy.

On the other hand, it might be even worse if they all went about choking back their bad feelings. There are few of us so insensitive that we don't realize when somebody is in a gloomy mood, and if he keeps still about it we are likely to wonder if he is annoyed with us. If we're not angry at anyone in particular, but just at the world in general, it is a good idea to announce it, then the people around us will know that the grumpiness isn't their doing.

So the only objective worth while in this problem of bad moods is to learn not to have any, and this is not as close to pursuing the unattainable as one might think at first glance. We must be full of a fervent desire for success, we must have patience, determination, and a willingness to work for what we want. We must forever keep in mind that it is our inside feelings we are aiming to change; we are really going to become a serene and pleasant person, not merely give the appearance of one.

My mother got a good deal of credit throughout her life for not indulging in unkind remarks about people, seldom losing her temper, worrying, getting upset, scolding. But those who knew her only superficially missed the significant thing about all this: she scarcely ever did any of those things because she didn't *feel* like doing them. It was a much bigger thing than it seemed to the casual observer. If she were alive today and I could ask her how she had achieved this condition, I rather doubt if she could tell me; I am not at all sure that she had to work at it. Not a do-gooder in the usual sense of the word, I think she did more good by quietly and unselfconsciously being herself than anyone I have ever known.

Without her here to tell us how to go about it, let's see what we can do toward thinking up some definite workable plan toward achieving pleasure, rather than pain, from our emotions. And let us stick primarily to the intimacy of the home, with emphasis on the husband-wife relation, for if we succeed there, we should be able to win everywhere.

If we're going to try to live comfortably and peaceably with others with a minimum of wrangling, one of the first things to abandon is the necessity of being "justly" treated in many small matters. If the members of your family are reasonably decent, considerate people, there is little doubt that, as they see it, you are being treated as fairly by them as they are by you. Since they see everything from their side of the fence, since their ideas and temperaments are, to some extent at least, different from yours, there can be no doubt that often each goes around feeling that he is the one who is getting the thin end of it.

While I think it is wise, if one likes peace, to give in quietly in many little things without making a fuss, I do believe in doing as I please in the things that concern nobody but me. I would not, for instance, wear a dress which my family disliked even if I thought it pretty and becoming; after all, they have to look at it. On the other hand, I do my gardening barefooted, no matter what anyone thinks about it. Nobody has to follow me around and look at me while I'm working, and I feel that it is exclusively my affair how I dress, or undress, when I'm alone.

The business of giving in can go too far. I don't understand why a husband or wife will permit the other to make a habit of being rude and unpleasant to him (or her) in the presence of others. I realize that it is expecting too much never to have some hot and hasty words through long married years, but there are people who embarrass everyone by being disagreeable to their husbands or wives at a social gathering. This may happen once in a long while, of course, to almost anybody, but there are those who make a practice of it, and I am inclined to feel that the victim is as responsible as the culprit. It is as embarrassing to innocent bystanders to see one person submitting to this treatment as to hear the other dealing it out. And easy enough to avoid, I should think, particularly if you start when the performance is just beginning to develop into a habit. It seems to me that all one has to do is to refuse to go anywhere or have guests if the other can't manage to be decently courteous.

The first few years of married life have the reputation of being the most difficult. I believe this is supposed to be true primarily because it takes time to get used to someone else's temperament and do the necessary adjusting. To my mind the biggest hurdle, if you are in love with each other and let's hope you are, is the very fact that you are; you start out by thinking the other is a good deal more wonderful than is likely, and there is a certain amount of disillusionment ahead. Worse than that, the other one thinks that you are just short of perfect, and unfortunately has almost got you convinced that he's right.

In this event, you have a double job ahead of you. Not only, for a short time anyway, must you try to be as perfect as the other believes, but you also have to be as wonderful as you yourself have decided you are. You can't swing either one, so it's rough going.

One regrettable result of this is that the one who tries harder and longer to stay on the pedestal is likely to start a pretty inclusive job of spoiling the other. He probably can't keep it up, in which case there will be some difficult moments. If he does continue for quite a while, the time will almost surely come when he begins to resent the whole setup. Here is this person who expects and usually gets far more than is equable; it makes him furious and he forgets it is his own doing.

I still stand by what I said a few paragraphs back about not putting up a fight for "justice" in the case of dozens of small, unimportant things. But I am constantly shocked when a husband or wife accepts an uneven deal, not liking it, complaining perhaps, but still doing nothing about it. It isn't so much that the thing in itself is particularly important; the worst aspect is that the one who is getting the biggest and juiciest piece of pie is likely to become an offensively spoiled and selfish person.

If my husband and I, let us say, were both especially fond of resting in a certain chair in the living room, I might always leave it vacant for him and not mind at all, provided he didn't know that I preferred it. But if he did know this and nevertheless took care to grab it, I would mind very much. Such lack of consideration staring me in the face, day in, day out, from the man who had set out to cherish me, would be a bitter dose to swallow.

I believe we should give some profound thought to which of our rights we are going to stand up for and which let pass. With my temperament, I need to feel that the people I live with mean to be decently considerate, and I would try not to be so selfless that I would first spoil them and later resent the fact that they were spoiled. Also, I would hate to have our friends disliking my husband because he was selfish. And, since I'm not an angel, let's add to all this nobility that I would like to hang onto just a few preferences for my own sweet sake.

Beyond that, and for one's peace of mind and pleasurable living, I think the intelligent thing in most cases is quietly to abandon one's less important desires. I can't give examples of

what I mean, because what is trifling to one person may not
be to another. The main thing, I suppose, is to put as many
things as possible in the unimportant category.

Here is one thing Fred did (or rather didn't do), which
took me a long time to get over minding. It is so insignificant
that, actually, I am ashamed to tell it, but I think we need it as
an example of how uncomfortable a grown person can make
herself over nothing at all.

Before dinner we had cocktails, Fred in his big chair and me
on the couch. Then I would go to the kitchen and, as I put
the last dish on the table, would say that dinner was ready. We
ate in the living room in the winter, on the porch in the summer. In either case Fred was close by and couldn't miss the
fact that dinner was on the table.

Now, I happen to be a person who can stop anything I'm
doing at a second's notice. If I'm planning to go to bed at ten
o'clock, as likely as not I'll stop reading in the middle of a
sentence when the clock strikes ten. But Fred always had to
finish things—a sentence if he was reading, certainly, and
probably a paragraph.

Well, for a longer time than I care to remember it provoked
me that Fred didn't jump up and come to the table when I
said dinner was ready. Sometimes it seemed to me that he
was going to finish the chapter, if not the book. Something in
me, however, must have told me that my annoyance was out
of proportion to the sin, because I didn't say anything about
it, and this was in the early days before I had learned to keep
still about my small preferences.

So I suffered in silence. Then I thought up tricks, for it

was against my principles to get irritated at anything and I especially disapproved of that feeling when I was sitting down to eat. My first strategy was to announce dinner a few minutes before it was ready, and that worked beautifully on those rare occasions when Fred and the dinner managed to arrive at the table simultaneously. But when they didn't, I ran into trouble because Fred, too, had his little quirks, and one of them was that he didn't like to wait. So if dinner wasn't on the table at the split second when he was ready to sit down, he thought up some little errand to do and that threw the whole performance out of gear.

My next trick was to say that dinner was ready and then I would go and do a little errand. That didn't work at all, because Fred just assumed that I wasn't ready after all and so went on with his reading until the dinner began to get cold. Next, I thought: Well, I'll just sit down and begin to serve (there were only us two) and Fred won't like that; it will seem rude, and he'll say something and then I'll answer most amiably, "Why, I called you, honey, when I put it on."

But Fred had always been a little absent-minded; he didn't seem to notice anything amiss and, since the food was invariably too hot for him anyway, there was no help in that department. I gave up; that is, I gave up being annoyed. For many years I called him to dinner, then sat down and began to serve. He never knew that there had been a problem.

I said I was ashamed of this, but in a way I'm not, for the basis of annoyance was never the fact that I had to wait a few minutes; I don't mind waiting practically indefinitely if I'm not standing on a cold, windy corner. What I minded was the seeming lack of consideration, and I think we are justified in feeling upset if the people who are supposed to love us are inconsiderate. But I am ashamed that it took me so long to realize that what seems thoughtless to one person doesn't to another. I should have reminded myself that Fred was a considerate person (which he was), and I believe that it is exactly here that all of us are constantly making a big mistake. What we take for thoughtlessness is simply a different point of view. Once we make up our minds that the people whose behavior affects us in dozens of little things each day at least want to be fair and decent, we have a good start on the path of peace. I don't mean peace merely in the absence of quibbling and grumbling, but peace in our hearts.

Take some trifling fault of a husband or wife that is utterly meaningless unless it disturbs us. If it does, there is a choice of two things we can try to do to get rid of the annoyance. One is to "cure" the other person of the "bad" habit; the other is to learn not to mind it. My conviction is that nine times out of ten, and probably ninety-nine out of one hundred, it is easier to change ourselves than somebody else. The first step is a recognition of the fact that a change is desirable and then go about accomplishing it.

I doubt if there is a more formidable job in the world than that of living successfully with others, and the difficulty is at its height when it is husband and wife we are considering. Why? As I said earlier, assuming that they are in love, they have started out with an exaggerated conception of each other's virtues. As disillusionment sets in, trouble arises. It is quite a shock when the man who has gone on record as adoring you snaps at you the first time. Then one day he will say something critical, and at last you know the bitter truth: he thinks you are somewhat less than perfect.

There is one thing about getting married that we are so used to we don't give it any thought. Here you are today, a relatively free person; you may live with your family, in which case there is a give-and-take relationship. You have learned to be more or less considerate in such things as not staying in the bathroom a long time, being late to meals, keeping your room tidy. But in most respects you are free. You don't even have to tell anyone where you are going if you don't care to; you are going "out."

Then you get married and it is almost unbelievable what this signifies, and astounding that anyone can bear it. It means that from now on, for the rest of your life, almost always you will eat breakfast and dinner with the same person. Nearly every penny you spend will to some degree be partly another's affair. However much you'd like to quit your job and do something you'd like better and live on less money, you can't. No matter how much you'd welcome not bothering to get dinner and just have some crackers and milk, you have to cook. If you'd like to go to a concert with some friend, since your husband or wife doesn't really care for music, you can't for fear of hurt feelings. Everything you buy, everything you eat, everything you do is largely connected with one other person. Possibly you can't even go to bed when you feel like it.

Maybe that seems all right to you, but my guess is that, however much you may love some friend, you wouldn't dream of trying to live with him under such circumstances, for life, for better or worse. To me it is simply amazing that so many of us weather the storm.

But we do accept the situation and accustom ourselves to it. Because it is so universally done, the over-all picture doesn't offend us. The things that do aggravate us are the hundreds of avoidable trifles that crop up, day in, day out, year upon year. If, for a few weeks, you kept a notebook handy and jotted down everything about which some unpleasantness arose, all the odds and ends which rubbed you the wrong way, my guess is that you would be surprised at the repetition. After all, each person has only his own peculiar kind of annoying traits, and his individual quota of the kinds of things that irritate him.

It therefore turns out that the job of putting an end to the various disturbances that make your day a distressing, or at least a vaguely unsatisfactory one, is not nearly as difficult or complicated as it might seem at first glance. If you are in a hurry to find peace, you might tackle the whole lot at once and make up your mind to let none of these things get under your skin in the future; if you are of another kind of temperament, you might accomplish more by choosing only one undesirable thing some member of your family does and train yourself not to mind it. If you are at all sensitive and reasonably honest with yourself, you know, too, some of the things you do and say that bring out the worst in your husband or wife. You can probably cut down on these.

You can certainly forestall a number of petty arguments. If you know that your wife hates to be contradicted, why not restrain yourself? It may bother you a little to hear her announce that John got drunk the last time he came to dinner, when you know perfectly well that it was the next to the last time, but if you value peace, why don't you let her make the statement unchallenged? It probably isn't of much importance to anybody which time it was.

No doubt you have heard stories of someone going all to pieces when he misses his bus, not because of that small inconvenience, but because annoyances of many kinds have hounded him all day and this last one is just more than he can bear. This happens to us all the time; the people in your office suffer because you have had a quarrel with your wife, and on another day she is made miserable because of the aggravations in your office. We hold back our grievances, then take them out later on some innocent bystander.

Lately many people have begun relying on tranquilizers, which seems a pity; it would be better to depend on ourselves, to learn to be serene by some method that will stand by us if we should mislay the bottle of pills.

Finally, let's have a look at a few more of those unwelcome emotions that have nothing to do with other persons, or with petty irritations. What are we searching for? What is it we need to make our lives pleasanter, not to say happier?

Lots of money? But do we know a single rich person who is noticeably happy? A trip around the world? Well, what will you do when you get back home again? The boss's job? But he looks harried and has ulcers. You're getting old? So are we all, and it isn't painful, once you get used to it. Beauty? It doesn't stand by you. Prestige? Trying to hang onto it is a wearing job. Success and recognition in your art? Try mastering the art of living.

Building your life is like making a pie. Your favorite is cherry, but you haven't any cherries, so you settle for apples. Here is the flour, but you are unfortunately out of lard, which in your opinion, makes the best crust. Well, all right, you will use bacon grease. Next, there's a calamity—the sugar bin is empty. Why not try honey? Besides being sweet it is supposed to have a lot of nutritive value. No cinnamon? Then use twice as much nutmeg and a little vanilla, why not? But you find that the vanilla bottle is empty, so how about some almond extract? Interesting to see what that will taste like.

So you make the pie—and you build your life—with make-shift ingredients, and it may happen that both will turn out better than they would have if you could have had exactly what you wanted.

V

"'What Do You Want?' Quoth God. 'Pay the Price and Take It.'"

In that homemade definition of happiness in the first chapter, I mentioned physical, mental, and emotional enjoyment, then boldly included the spirit. I didn't mean this in any religious sense, particularly not in any orthodox one. If you write about anything from the point of view of a Christian, for instance, you will exclude everyone who isn't a Christian, and surely we all have the wish and right to make a play for happiness, whatever our religion or lack of it.

So what do I mean by spirit? Well, I will start out by admitting that I don't know precisely what I do mean; it may be no more than mind or emotion at its highest and purest, but whatever it is we can call it spirit and try not to confuse it with any dogmatic meaning. It may even include physical pleasures (the five senses) at their loftiest. Many of us know what it is to get an uplift when we listen to certain passages of music which move us profoundly—a joy which seems in some way far above mere physical pleasure.

I remember a man I knew fairly well some years ago; he was a bachelor and managed to live almost exclusively for himself. He seemed to prefer to say a bad word about his friends rather than a good one. He would cheat you a little if he could, would always contrive to help himself to the most comfortable chair and the biggest piece of pie. He rented desk space in some office, and a girl there was willing to take a letter from him now and then without charge, but she told him he would have to buy a stenographer's notebook. Rather than spend the money for one, he wrote his own letters. I have camouflaged him so thoroughly that he will never recognize this portrait, yet in essence it is true.

But he loved fine music so much that when he listened to it or spoke of it or hummed something or, I believe, just thought about it, letting a tune run through his head, he became quite another person. His usual expression was one of ill temper; his speaking voice was irritable, but when he was contemplating music, his voice became quiet and sympathetic, and his expression was almost that of a peaceful, happy saint. That, I suppose, is spirit, and it may come to life, then, through the medium of one of the five senses.

Our eyes can accomplish this for us too. The Grand Canyon did it for me and so, above all, did the Russian steppe. I believe vast mountains are supposed to make Man feel how insignificant he is, but the Grand Canyon and the steppe affected me just the opposite; I felt that to be only a tiny speck in the midst of such magnificence made me a part of it, a little more than nothing. Several times I was in a sleigh, riding on the steppe, and saw the sun go down and the stars come out and the moon rise as we rode on and on and on, and ever since then, when someone pulls me to his picture window and says proudly, "Look! You can see so-and-so many miles," I pretend to be impressed but I want to answer, "Pooh! I have seen all the way to infinity." It was awesome, and awe, I suppose, has something in it which we may call spirit.

Just last night I looked at the new moon from an upstairs window and, to add to its charm, there were a few bare branches outlined against the sky. That thin sliver of brightness always moves me profoundly; I feel it pulling me and, silly though it sounds, I want badly to take it in my arms and cuddle it.

Fragrance can carry us right into the clouds, and for me the sense of touch can, too. I don't mean velvet or wood or even the satin of a rose or peony, although if you shut your eyes and let yourself go you're likely to feel fairly lofty. But it's the feel of the good earth which transports me to some other kingdom. Just any old soil won't do; it has to be the right texture, the right dampness and dryness. It must, in short, be the kind that earthworms deign to live in and that plants demand if they are going to fulfill their destiny.

I can't remember ever being uplifted by a taste but (forgive me, Carrie Nation) I do often seem to overflow with tolerance and goodwill to all after a Daiquiri.

So much for the five senses and, considering that I expected almost no help from them, I don't think I did badly.

When I settle down to it, I'm surprised to find it difficult, if not impossible, to tie up the mind with spirit. Is the mind as cold and reasonable (or unreasonable) as it seems to be? Are the novels and poems and high sentiments that move and profoundly stir us written only with the mind or, in part at least, with the emotions and spirit?

Does it matter? Well, I suppose so, but since I can't figure it out I'm going to pretend that it doesn't. And perhaps that is precisely the point; perhaps spirit is so closely related to, and mixed through, every part of us that we can't separate it from the things about ourselves that we can enumerate and analyze. The senses and the mind are carrying us constantly into emotion, and perhaps that is what spirit is: emotion at its highest level. Love is an emotion, and I suspect that most people would tell us that all-embracing love is a spiritual concept.

Where does this land us? At least I think we can still hang onto our definition of happiness, for if we can manage to make the best of our five senses, our mind, and our emotions, it seems to lead us straight to the kind of joy that, for want of a better term, we may call spiritual. This is an advantage for those who feel that happiness is too crude a thing, hardly worth aiming at, if it is limited to the physical. At the same time, those who shy away from the word "spiritual" can simply refuse to use it in connection with those exalted moments and peaceful hours, the value of which they probably admit.

One path that any discussion of the spiritual phase of our lives must explore—especially if we're concerned about serenity and well-being as elements of happiness—is the one marked "morality" and "integrity." Can we be happy if we consciously, or even unconsciously, uphold dishonesty and hypocrisy? Let me try to point out some of the most common, innocent-seeming, but detrimental circumstances and attitudes.

As with so much of our behavior, childhood and the relationship between parents and children are particularly strategic in molding our concepts of truth and decency. In my observation, the sin that most parents can bear least in their children is lying. This seems a most peculiar fault to lay so much stress on, since everybody abandons the truth occasionally, including those very parents who go all to pieces if poor little Johnny, backed to the wall, looks them in the eye and declares he didn't do it. Children have such lively imaginations that through the early years they often can't distinguish between fancy and reality. Once my four-year-old niece put an imaginary baby on a sofa and covered it with a blanket which didn't exist; the baby went to sleep and presently someone came into the room and sat down on it. My niece screamed with horror and was quieted only when my sister rescued the imaginary baby, rocked and patted it, and showed the child that it wasn't hurt. It would have been useless to try to explain to her that there wasn't any baby there, for there was; she had put it there herself.

I should think that until children are old enough to distinguish clearly between truth and the accepted untruths that everyone indulges in when it's convenient, they must be confused, since, for them, it is considered such a sin to lie, while for the grownups it is obviously run-of-the-mill. Probably they can hardly wait until they are old enough to tell the truth only when they're in the mood.

Children hear Mother call up the office and say Daddy is sick, when there's not a thing in the world wrong with him; in fact, he's feeling extra good because he's going fishing. And what a big one that is—Mother telling Mrs. So-and-so that she's simply delighted she came, when Mother said two minutes ago that she wished to heavens she wouldn't. And the children catch Daddy in some whoppers too, telling Mrs. Brown that Mother isn't home when she just this minute went upstairs; Daddy certainly saw her go, because he was talking to her while she went.

My mother didn't expect her children to be any better than she was; in fact, she didn't expect them to be as good since they were so much younger and she knew that it takes time to adjust one's values. A rather curious fact is that she didn't know how to lie. At one time, when we were all grown, we made an effort to teach her—that is, to say to this one or that one who telephoned us that we weren't at home. She had heard us do this for each other and had made no comment, nor had she given us any feeling that she disapproved, and therefore if she happened to answer the telephone when there was some bore we were trying to avoid, we would say to her, "If it's So-and-so, tell him I'm not here."

She tried to oblige but she sounded most unconvincing,

and if the pest already suspected our feelings toward him, he probably guessed the truth. I don't believe her confused manner came from thinking it was wrong to tell that kind of lie, for if she had thought so, she wouldn't have done it. I think it was simply that it seemed a little fantastic to her to say you weren't home when you were there in the room with her.

One day the doorbell rang and Mother answered it. The caller was a man I avoided on the telephone, and when he asked if I was home, Mother hesitated and then turned to me and said, "Ruth, it's So-and-so; are you here?" (I was close by, although the man couldn't see me.) After that we decided to manage without her cooperation.

I never heard her express an opinion on the subject of lying, but I remember that she told us that sometimes her father, after listening to some doubtful tale, would remark quietly, "Wouldn't it be a pity if there wasn't a word of truth in that?" I can only guess at Mother's attitude. I suppose it was ethical to some extent but, reducing it to its simplest terms, I imagine it would have been something like this: However unwelcome the truth may be, I'd rather face it than run. For one whose over-all approach to life was "I give thanks in all things," facing any truth, big or little, probably wasn't much of a chore.

Each child is going to live in a world where the truth is being constantly stretched to fit the occasion, and he is going to think crookedly enough about things without our giving him a false start. In the dealings between two nations he is going to find out that it is vile if the other country breaks an agreement, but if his own country does it, it is for an understandable and probably even a noble reason. At the very worst, a good excuse. A spy, he learns, is a person who lives a lie, and the enemy's spies are despicable while his country's spies are heroes. This would confuse even a grownup if he stopped to think about it.

Every child is going to live in a society in which almost nobody is horrified at the commercials that are beamed at them all day long from radio and television. Your youngsters will discover that the young man who implies that neither your life nor his will be worth living if you don't drink the coffee or eat the mustard he is at the moment recommending, would say the same thing about any other brand the very next week if he should happen to go to work for a competitor. Toothpaste manufacturers mislead millions when they say that their brands will help to prevent cavities. Makers of breakfast foods falsely promise our children that the stuff they are selling will make youngsters strong and healthy.

All this doesn't mean that, because our child must live in a world of misrepresentation, we should deliberately teach him to lie so that he will become accustomed to it. We don't have to, anyhow, for he will learn it soon enough without our guidance. But I don't understand those parents who practically force a child to lie prematurely by putting him on the spot, taking him firmly by the arm and saying, "Look me in the eyes, Johnnie. Did you do that? Now don't lie to me."

Unless Johnnie is a pretty bad egg he will probably come through well enough, whether he tells the truth this time or not. As he grows up he will find out when it is acceptable to lie and when it is dishonorable. In other words, he'll soon learn (perhaps unfortunately) to conform and live by other people's standards. What those standards are to be is up to us, however; remember, each of us has a large measure of freedom to choose our own—and, above all, the freedom to think for ourselves. And it's the best heritage we can give our children. We can also teach them to let those around them think for *themselves*. That will contribute to their own happiness, for it will make for a relaxed atmosphere. In other words, teach them not to be naggers.

Let us say that the worst thing you have to put up with is somebody's nagging. There is no doubt in your mind that it is the one who nags who ought to mend his ways, and by all means cure him if you can. But maybe he can't stop or doesn't even want to. Probably it hasn't occurred to him to try to, and besides I doubt if he calls his excellent advice nagging.

If you are going in for happiness in the sense in which I mean it, you will probably have to more or less abandon the words "ought to" in connection with everybody except perhaps yourself. Try to forget about justice; it is true that no one ought to nag you, but actually the only undesirable thing about it, for you, is that it irritates you. So change yourself, stop being annoyed and do without justice, trading it in for a pleasant atmosphere.

A simple rule for foiling the nagger is never to give him an argument. No matter how absurd his suggestion may seem to you, don't try to enlighten him. Anyway, there is small chance that he would pay any attention to your intelligent comments. If he flies into a rage at getting no reaction and if peace is your goal, you will probably have to think up some kind of an answer and not just ignore him; you might count to one thousand and then murmur politely, "Yes, dear, perhaps I should" (or shouldn't, as the case may be). If it has been your custom to react with spirit, it might be safer to taper off gradually, for if you become too humble too suddenly, he might think you are sick and begin nagging you about taking care of your health.

Now what if you are the culprit, the one who does the nagging? In that case it is possible that you don't see so clearly any necessity for mending your ways. It's a pretty safe bet that you have never thought of yourself as a nagger; when you advise people you are simply telling them this and that for their own good, aren't you? There are two things you might ask yourself: One, do people follow my suggestions? Two, do they seem to be irritated at my interference? If the answers are, respectively, no and yes, those around you might be happier if you stopped "helping" them. I think that you will also be happier yourself; it must be frustrating to hand around a lot of good advice with meager results.

I have to work hard at trying to abandon bad habits and form good ones, but I have never had to kill the urge to tell other people how to behave, because I have never been tempted in that respect and I'd like to tell you a story about that. Shortly after Fred and I were married we went to a rather large party at my brother's home, and we asked Fred's niece, Helen, whom I had met only once or twice, to meet us there.

During the evening Helen came up to me with Fred in tow and said, "Ruth, how could you let Fred come to a party dressed like this?"

I glanced at my new husband, who looked normally clothed

to me and very nice, and then at Helen with, I suppose, a question in my eyes.

Fred laughed and said, "Look, Helen, Ruth hasn't even noticed that I have on dancing pumps with a business suit. If she had, she wouldn't see anything wrong with it. If she knew it wasn't proper, she wouldn't give a damn. And even if she didn't like the idea, she wouldn't mention it because she'd think it was my business what I wore and not hers."

Maybe I could give you a pointer or two if I had attained this particular attitude by overcoming an inclination to advise other people about what they should wear, and could tell you just how to go about curing yourself of that habit, but it is my good fortune that I have never cared in the least what anybody wears at any time. Probably if someone I liked very much went around in something I thought hideous and unbecoming, I would drop a hint but so far I haven't been tempted.

We live in the country. Once, on a hot afternoon, our weekend guests were starting home, back to Long Island. Jim (we'll call him) had on a fresh white shirt, comfortably open at the neck, and his wife insisted that he put on a necktie. Finally he gave in but he wasn't happy about it.

Why did she care? Why isn't it physically, morally, mentally, humanly impossible to mind if people see you without a necktie on a hot day? Or even on a cold one. Might they run into a friend, and would the absence of a necktie spoil the relationship? No, impossible. And I refuse to believe that she could care what strangers think. She is a kind woman; does she fear that some little boy will like the way her husband looks and twenty years later get a job in a bank and one hot day will go to work without a tie and get fired and maybe his children will go hungry and eventually starve to death? Of course I'm being utterly ridiculous, but don't you have to be ridiculous when you set out to think up a reason for a woman to insist that a man wear a necktie if he doesn't want to?

What has this trifle (if it is a trifle) got to do with our subject, which is filling our days with peace and serenity? Is it such a hardship for a man to wear a tie to please his wife? No, and if Jim had felt agreeable about it and had said to himself, "Well, all right, Jennie has a thing about ties so I'll wear one to please her," that would have been a kind gesture, and Jennie might even have been so touched by his thoughtfulness that she would have told him to take it off, but, no, I rather doubt that. Jim is intelligent and thinks for himself. He knew that Jennie's insistence had no reason back of it, that it was simply her need to conform. It is a rather pitiable thing, Jim thinks, to follow rules without reason, and is going too far when you insist that others conform, too. Besides not wanting to wear a tie, the attitude irks him.

There is still more to it than that. When people live together, particularly husband and wife, there is of course a great deal of adjusting to be done. In the dozens of things which concern both of them, there have to be compromises, even sacrifices. This is unavoidable and to a greater or lesser degree will at times interfere with the harmony of the household.

I should think, then, that, not in the interest of justice but to preserve peace, the wise thing is to leave the other person

alone in everything he does which doesn't affect you. If you
presented that argument to Jennie, she would be capable of
saying that it distressed her for her husband not to wear a tie
and therefore it *did* affect her. She hasn't a logical mind. Let
us say she likes to go to bed at ten o'clock and Jim prefers to
sit up until twelve. Maybe he reads quietly or maybe he keeps
the radio on at full blast. In either case, Jennie can't go to
sleep because she thinks he ought to go to bed. The strange
part is that she wouldn't see that it was reasonable for her to
insist that he turn the radio low, or off, but unreasonable for
her to interfere with his sitting up and reading. She doesn't
see the big gap between standing up for her rights and expecting others to humor her quirks. And even the former can
be carried too far if peace is our goal.

The tie controversy on that Sunday afternoon could have
developed into a man-size quarrel if Jim had decided to stand
up for his rights. Even as it was, he gave in with bad grace
and our friends started off with both of them disgruntled,
leaving us feeling sorry for them. It had been a particularly
enjoyable weekend, for we were fond of both of them, but
that incident, at the end of it, was like finishing an excellent
meal with unpalatable dessert and inferior coffee. It left a bad
taste in our mouths.

Skipping for the moment grim things such as doing our
duty, making a living, being our Brother's Keeper, I suppose
we can assume that our activities are successful insofar as
they are giving us real satisfaction. By "real" I mean some
kind of inner glow, or peace, or exhilaration which stays with
us.

Let's have a look at those activities about which we have a choice. What we do with our money is an ever-recurring issue, and there is a world of difference between the money we must spend to pay the rent and buy the necessary food and the money with which we can do as we please. Even in rent and food there is an element of choice; we can live in a cheaper apartment perhaps, and spend the money we save for something more frivolous. And we can eat less costly food, buy less liquor, and have an expensive coat or another pair of shoes.

My guess is that you already realize that you make all such choices constantly, unless you are so rich that you don't have to choose and can have everything. But most of us have to give up one thing in order to have another, and we may do it almost unconsciously and often for the wrong reason, wrong in the sense that if a choice is made without serious and thoughtful consideration we may do ourselves some actual injury.

I wrote the last paragraphs before I had read Vance Packard's *The Waste Makers* and was only hazily conscious of the tremendous strides the merchants and advertisers have made toward doing our thinking and choosing for us without our knowing it. I will let my words stand as they are, however, even though, by the time you read them, things may have come to such a sorry pass that my words may sound like a tactless joke.

Last winter I met a woman who had awakened from this trance of frantic spending in order to "keep up." I talked at a garden club, and it turned out to be one of those affairs at which, for one thing, I was probably the only woman who wasn't wearing a hat.

On this occasion the woman (about forty or forty-five years old) who drove me home after the meeting opened her heart to me. She suddenly said, "For some reason I can talk to you and I've got to confide in somebody or I'll burst. You see this coat I have on—"

I glanced at it; until then I hadn't noticed it, but now I realized that it was just about the loveliest one I had ever seen. Not mink, something grander than that, I thought, and at any rate prettier.

"It's beautiful," I murmured.

"Yes, it is and I hate it. It was much too expensive for me, but all our crowd you saw today began to appear one after another in gorgeous coats and I couldn't stand it. I looked around and found this one and telephoned my husband and practically issued an ultimatum: I would have this coat or else! He came through, and I've had it on about four times and I loathe it. Our whole setup is like that—living above our means. I just had to tell somebody."

We drove in silence for a little while. I was trying to think of something to say that might, somehow, do her a little good; the best I could manage was:

"The only thing I can tell you is that I don't believe you need to worry. Probably most of those other poor women have the same values you had and don't even realize that they are pretty shoddy and very childish, but you do know now, and I'm sure you've got what it takes to carry on from there."

I felt sorry for this woman, but it was the others who needed any pity I had to spare. They probably were completely unconscious of the fact that the coats they wore and the houses they owned (possibly heavily mortgaged) had been bought primarily for the satisfaction of "keeping up," and in terms of personal pleasure and satisfaction to themselves were not worth the price.

And the lower we go in the financial scale, the more regrettable it becomes to see people unconsciously sacrificing something they could really enjoy (such as peace of mind) for something bought merely to show their friends they can afford it. It's not easy to squeeze out a tear for the man who can't afford an expensive car but feels he has to splurge, yet he is just as pitiable as the woman whose old winter coat is plenty good enough and even prettier than the new one which she buys because she is ashamed to wear the same one so long. Maybe she liked it very much once, but thinks that she personally has grown tired of it. Why should she? She put it away somewhere in April and hasn't even seen it for six or seven months. Unless she is a fickle woman I should think she would greet it like an old and valued friend who has been away for the summer. To me, one of the advantages of living in a climate which has drastic changes in temperature is that one can have a complete new wardrobe two or three times a year, simply by opening a closet and getting out last season's garments.

About fifteen years ago one of my sisters gave me a good black cloth coat with a pretty, soft collar. It had belonged to her mother-in-law, who had worn it for a few years, then had given it to my sister, who wore it a year or two for second best, then gave it to her daughter, who also used it for second best for a couple of years.

Now it was offered to me. Surprisingly, it didn't look at all worn (at least, it didn't to me, although I admit that my eyesight isn't perfect), and I adopted it for my best coat. Another sister made unfriendly remarks about it as the years piled up, but I had developed quite a fondness for it and ignored her. After eight years or so, I carelessly went with her when she shopped for a coat for herself and somehow she manipulated things so that I also came home with one.

I did like the new one better than the black one, but as far as my own pleasure was concerned I didn't need a new coat. I'm not entirely out of touch with reality, however; I suspect there aren't very many women who could happily wear somebody else's old coat that long. I'll even admit that probably they would want a new one for their own sakes and not just because they cared what people might be thinking. As to my friends, I doubt if any of them realized that I'd had that coat so long and, if they did, I'm convinced they didn't care. As time went on, the sixth year, the seventh, the eighth, not one of them stopped speaking to me or asking me to dinner. And now no one treats me a bit better than before I got the new coat. If they talked about the old one behind my back, I didn't know it, and if people find it fascinating to discuss my old clothes, I'd be the last one to want to do them out of that pleasure.

At one time in my life I bought and wore beautiful and expensive clothes. This was accidental; I had a job with an elegant Fifth Avenue store, and toward the end of each season they sold off all the garments on hand to their employees at an absurdly low price. I was head of the wholesale bookkeeping department and therefore in a position to do favors for the buyers, so when these sales were due, I was often offered some choice specimens. I wasn't especially clothes conscious, but I suppose in one's twenties it is next to impossible to be offered a glamorous hundred-dollar garment for $4.50 and not grab it. The result was that not only was I dressed beautifully all the time, but so were my sisters and friends.

I'm grateful for that experience; every young woman should be able to dress elegantly and expensively for a year or so just to find out how unstable and unreliable is the "happiness" it gives her. Not only didn't those clothes bring me anything beyond the fleeting pleasure of enjoying their attractiveness, but they seemed to frighten the young men who might (who knows?) have proposed to me if they hadn't been sure that I was too expensive for them. Whereas I am just about the cheapest bargain, in terms of money, that any man could ask for.

My natural lack of interest in material things was accentuated when I spent a year in Russia with the Quakers doing famine relief work. Somehow, when you are in close touch with a large orphanage (the parents had died of starvation), where the children decorate their rooms with the bright-colored labels from tomato cans, sent from America, the lavishness of things revolts you somewhat when you get back home. One way of spending money that insults my intelligence is to pay a disproportionately high price for something. I recall that a small dish of peas in a restaurant I was taken to once cost more than a bushel of fresh-picked ones.

Then there's the whole business of persuasion by advertising, which Mr. Packard brought home to me. In a newspaper strike which happened just before Christmas one year in New York, the papers were said to have lost several million dollars in advertising. If you told that to the man from Mars, unacquainted with our behavior, and explained to him that this advertising was primarily meant to tell people where to go to buy what, mostly for Christmas presents, he would probably exclaim, "Oh dear, then I suppose Christmas was bleak, since nobody knew where to go to buy what they wanted." He would, of course, have been mistaken, for, deficient as we may all be in brain power, we can gather a few wits together and find our way to a store to buy some presents, even when we have no advertising to guide us.

Speaking of Christmas and presents, I like the *spirit* of giving, whether it is of one's time, one's self, or even merely of something one buys. But, prevalent as the *act* is, among adults actual giving is practically non-existent; it is almost universally a trading, a giving back. Recently I had a fine opportunity to give something to a friend which she could never have had otherwise and which had been an impossible-to-achieve dream for her. She kept saying, "How can I ever repay you? In a whole lifetime I can never pay you back."

I tried my utmost to make her see that it wasn't a trade; a gift, I said, isn't something which has to be paid for, even with gratitude. She grasped this with her mind, but I'm afraid she is thoroughly contaminated with the current meaning of giving and will always feel indebted to me. And I am sorry.

Almost everyone gets satisfaction, pleasure, a spurt of happiness, out of helping somebody—just anybody. If you lose your way while driving and stop someone on the road to ask directions, notice how eager he is to be of help, and how he seems to regret it if he can't be. "I don't know—I'm sorry," he will say, and he obviously is.

Any man, a woman even if she seems in a hurry, a school-girl who may be a little shy—all do their best, and a boy is obviously delighted to give you directions, and usually knows, too. Even a policeman enters in with enthusiasm, although he must get dozens of requests in a day.

Get into real trouble and you will find out, not necessarily who your friends are, but what pleasure it is to most people to give time and energy to help anyone. On the other hand, if they were required to do it they might not care for it much; it then wouldn't be presenting a gift, but would merely be performing a duty.

When we give, whether we are prompted by sympathy, or love, or pity, or just for the pleasure of helping someone or even of feeling important, it is an enjoyable sensation, and I see nothing against keeping an eye out for opportunities to lend a helping hand. At times the satisfaction may even amount to moments of spiritual exaltation. Even here, though, we must be aware of some pitfalls.

There are several categories of people who spend a good deal of time doing for others. There are those who have empathy, and, as I understand this word, it means the quality of temporarily and involuntarily putting yourself in another's place to such an extent that you almost are that other person for the time being. I happen to be very closely acquainted with a person who has empathy, and have thus had a chance to watch it operate. We will call this friend of mine John. He got a bad toothache one day because he had seen a child on the street with one, and, as soon as he realized why he got it, it went away. He once let a twelve-year-old boy drive his car, because for the moment he was a little boy who was simply dying to drive. The child ran into a pole, wrecked the car, and John was taken to the hospital. I could tell you many more tales.

The result is that John spends a great deal of time doing good. It delights him when he can fix up somebody's troubles, but of course he is often upset because there are more troubles around than he can fix. Everything considered, I would say that the person with empathy is kind and lovable but not to be envied.

There are people who do good because they feel guilty. Some of these have more money than they need and can't help knowing that a lot of people haven't enough, so they set about giving some of theirs away. Not all of these people are multimillionaires but some of them are, and it would be interesting to know how many millions (or even how many hundred thousands) one can have left in the bank and not still feel guilty.

There are those who are unhappy and hope that doing good will alter that; we have sort of taken care of them. And there are, perhaps, some saints, but so few that we can skip them.

Now if you have empathy or if you are a saint, you have no problem, because whether it makes you happy or vice versa you're going to be constantly involved with other people's problems. But if you are just an everyday person, I doubt if setting out to live for others is going to bring you happiness.

Quite the contrary. I believe that if you want to lead a happy life (or, if that is too big an order, a pleasant, peaceful, serene one), you must, in a certain very real sense, think of yourself first. This happens to be what we all do practically all of the time, and take for granted, and yet it sounds shocking when we say it in connection with the pursuit of happiness.

Let's broaden the conception a little and for "self" substitute "immediate family." Because the man who works all day at a job and the woman who works at home, together supporting and caring for the children they've brought into the world, are, in a slightly broader sense, working for and thinking of themselves—that is, their own. There are a few hours in the evening and some on Saturday and Sunday which may be devoted to others. But don't forget that if you go to church you do it, presumably, to save your own soul, so don't give yourself a good mark for that.

Interestingly enough, if you do work for your own happiness and achieve it, everyone who comes in contact with you will enjoy you more and therefore be better off because you are happy. If you are busy building your own pleasant life, you have no time to criticize others. You are more relaxed, more fun to be with; your sense of humor is in good working order, and you are a do-gooder in the best sense without even trying.

I saw a cartoon the other day: a despondent-looking man was gazing out of a picture window. Two women were seated in the middle of the room, and one was saying to the other, "He wants to help people but he doesn't know how." I found that pathetic. From one motive or another, most of us would like to help people and some of us are miserable because we can do so little. A few even think it is impossible, or at least wrong, to be happy ourselves because of the suffering in the world.

Somebody said once that one starving baby called for as much compassion as a million starving babies, that in the second case, the situation is worse, but we feel so badly about one baby that we can't feel worse over a million. I don't know whether that is true or not, but this is surely true: If we are going to wait to try to find inner peace until everyone in the world is as well off as we are, physically, mentally, spiritually, then we can resign ourselves to going about with distressed faces and hearts every minute of our lives. A sorry prospect!

Once in a while we hear critical remarks to the effect that it is easy to take other people's troubles philosophically, but not our own. What a blessing it is, though, that the misfortunes of others (except those who are close to us) don't upset us unduly, for if they did, no one could ever have one moment free from distress. It may be ignoble to care more about our own toothache than about the millions who are miserable all over the world, but how long could we stand it if we suffered for others' misfortunes as acutely as we do for our own? God was merciful indeed when he spared us that capacity.

If by working only half of each day we can make enough money to pay for our necessities and a few modest luxuries, we can, if we wish, work the other half and use the money to buy necessities and luxuries for somebody else. We can, but we don't. And no one seems to think it is blameworthy to look out for number one when it is a matter of adding to material possessions or enjoyment in the nature of pleasure trips, recreation, or money in the bank. It would probably not embarrass you at all to tell your friends how hard you were working to save up money for a piano or a boat or a trip to Mexico, and I don't think it would occur to your friend to think how selfish you were, spending all that time and energy concentrating on your own good time.

But your friend might be shocked if you said in so many words that you were going to set out to find happiness by thinking only in terms of your own peace and serenity, that you weren't going to take anyone else into consideration. Your friend feels that you have become selfish and inconsiderate; you are going to be happy, by heck, no matter whom it hurts, but naturally it doesn't mean that at all.

And then: how can you set out to be happy with the world in such a mess? Well, how can you go to the theater, listen to music, take a trip, eat dessert, with the world in such a mess? But we can, and do, don't we?

Let's be a little fanciful and think of our daily lives, our thoughts, and behavior, as we do of our small vegetable patch. In the latter we spend time and energy to make things grow, both for our own sakes and for that of the people we are going to feed. It's true that we can't feed very many—our family, friends whom we invite for meals, and perhaps a neighbor whose cabbages were eaten by woodchucks—yet we don't decide not to have a garden because there are so many hungry people in the world whom we can't feed. As I see it, replacing dull or hectic or anxious hours with pleasant ones is even more helpful to those around us than serving them tender, fresh peas. Is it insensitive to cultivate your inner garden in a fashion that will at least keep you from being a depressing person to have around?

Then there are people who believe that we can't gain happiness by working for it; they claim it is a by-product. Ask them exactly what it is a by-product of, and they can't tell you. It seems that sometimes it is of one thing, sometimes another. It may be different for different people.

If it is true that almost all of us would like above all to be happy and the prospect of achieving it is as hit and miss as that, we are in a pickle indeed. Our helplessness is abysmal. One may be lucky and think he discovers that happiness for him is a by-product of playing the piano, and then he gets arthritis so badly that he can no longer use his fingers with any skill. Another finds it a by-product of her children and they get married and move far away.

If happiness is a by-product of anything at all outside yourself, then it is something you can lose. No, if you are going to get it and keep it, it must be something you can control. It has to stand by you, no matter what.

Recently someone wrote to me: "I would vote for a more active conception than the usual peace and serenity. I've observed an awful lot of people who seem to be happiest when in the midst of struggle and turmoil."

This seems to me to be making a complication out of a simple thing. I wouldn't say that peace and serenity are the opposite of struggle, which is a form of endeavor, and who wants to be static? But if by turmoil she means worry, fuss, anxiety, then people in the midst of turmoil are not what I would call happy. A person who can enjoy being alone, savoring an atmosphere of peace and quiet and who can also struggle in a hectic atmosphere, taking the fun and excitement and leaving the tension to others, is the person who knows how to be happy under all circumstances.

I was startled recently when a friend told me that she knew people who would damn this book because they believed that only shallow and stupid people could be happy. The idea was that the more one suffered, the more complex and interesting and intelligent one was.

I used to know people a long time ago who talked like that, but they were either very young or very frustrated; I was surprised that anyone was saying such things nowadays but I suppose I shouldn't have been, for there are still quite a few immature and frustrated people around. And I suppose there is nothing to say to them beyond telling them that if suffering makes them feel intellectual and superior, well, by all means suffer. But I feel about them as a little girl I know did about her father when she saw him for the first time without any clothes on; she didn't blame him for his peculiarities, she just felt sorry for him.

Another friend, giving me a helping hand, asked me if I was going to discuss the fact that we should recognize our limitations and also try to be aware of our unexploited capacities. "More and more," she wrote, "it is being generally admitted that not only are all people not equal, but they don't have equal opportunities either, and I am not just talking about the blind or the crippled."

I suppose that not recognizing our limitations would come

under the heading of pursuing the unattainable, and I have already put my foot down on that ambition. Trying to be aware of our capacities is surely a good constructive attitude, but I should think a person might make the mistake of concentrating too ardently on a meager one.

I am sorry, for instance, for the person who is determined to write, however many of his manuscripts have been rejected. If he writes for the pure love of the doing, he no doubt has a good time, whatever the consequences, but if it is rather a painful procedure (and it often is), and if, on top of that, his heart breaks when the manuscript is returned, I should think he would be better off doing something more enjoyable and productive. It is true that in a small handful of isolated cases a book turned down by a score of publishers has finally been printed and has become a best seller, and each author thinks, I suppose, that he may be in that category; if he has fun dreaming about this—splendid! But if he is consumed with minor agony, I'm sorry for him; it seems too bad to put too big a strain on our capacities.

Of late years there has been rather a to-do about people who discover, late in life, a modest ability to draw and paint, and this seems all to the good to me providing they don't take themselves too seriously and expect others to be impressed.

Hating waste, I am against gifts of ability lying around unused if they can add anything at all to anybody's pleasure, including, of course, one's own. Although doing the work we like and are fitted for isn't happiness, it goes a long way toward helping us find it, or at least keeps us in a pretty good humor while we're searching.

Years ago, I engaged a girl of nineteen to do simple clerical work in the office where I was employed. She was most inefficient, had a discontented expression, and was often sullen and disagreeable. Usually when I got hold of a girl who couldn't do the work well, I would get her transferred to another department, but no one would take on this girl.

One day I said to her, "You hate this work, don't you?"

"Yes, I loathe it."

"What would you like to do?"

"I don't know."

A few days later she said to me, "You look so pale. Are you sick?"

I was and she persuaded me to go to the restroom with her and, you may have guessed it: she was a born nurse and loved it. I could tell this from the way she took care of me for the next hour or so. I talked her mother into letting her go into training, and besides being outstandingly successful she became a very pleasant person.

We are not all of us so talented in some way that it comes through to our consciousness. But it is probably true that many of us could find some activity which would add pleasure to our lives, either as a job or a hobby, if we would look for it.

In general (although generalizations are fairly worthless), I would say that one can get more out of being a partaker than an onlooker. Not long ago a friend of ours was bemoaning the fact that he had bought tickets for a play to be given by amateurs, and that unfortunately he felt obliged to go since some of the actors were friends and acquaintances.

"I sing in the choral society," he went on, "and we give

performances and charge admission and expect our friends to sit through our performance. The only people who enjoy these plays and recitals are the ones on the stage."

But it is more serious than that. In the good old days, with no movies or television and fewer and less elaborate toys, children were compelled to use their own brains in order to find amusement. If we keep on the way we are now going and somewhere along the line don't finish it all with an atom bomb, I fervently hope there is no such thing as reincarnation; I don't see how I could enjoy myself with millions of robots and automatons going about doing nothing at all, ever, except pushing buttons. By the time I would get back here again, people probably won't even have to know which button to push; there will no doubt be a big one to control all the others, and one push on it and you'll get whatever you want. The fact that you won't have enough brains or incentive left to want anything that makes a particle of difference one way or the other won't matter. In fact, if you should push for an apple and get a pair of shoes, you probably won't even know the difference.

A lot has been said about the wisdom of living in the moment and to a great extent I go along with that. The past is gone, the future may never come for you, so get busy and have fun now. But I'm not one hundred per cent against living a little in the future. If you can give your all to the present and make each moment a happy one, you can ask for nothing better, but there are times when, squeeze as hard as you like, not a drop of enjoyment will come. This may happen when you are sitting in the dentist's chair or waiting for a bus—it will be different for each of us.

When we were in school out in Kansas there was nothing much more fun than debates, and one of the favorite topics was: "Resolved: that anticipation is more enjoyable than realization." I always preferred the affirmative and I still have a leaning toward it, which has to mean, then, that I sometimes like to abandon the present and live in the future. This is largely a matter of temperament; I know some people who avoid looking forward to something pleasant for fear it won't come out as they want it to and they will be disappointed. I am just the opposite; if it doesn't come off at all, at least I've had all that pleasure of looking forward to it. Besides, I'm a bit of an expert when it comes to imagining breath-taking activities, and no actual occurrence could ever quite come up to the splendors I can play around with before the event.

You probably remember that when you were young you indulged in daydreams where you did wondrous things and were admired and adored and goodness knows what. One outgrows this pastime, of course, but a year or so ago I accidentally made a valuable discovery. I am, in general, a very good sleeper, but one night I found myself wide awake for no discernible reason and tried some of the various mental tricks I had heard of, to no avail. So I decided to do a little childish daydreaming and glorify myself and thus at least have a good time. Well, that did it; I bored myself right to sleep. I've tried it a number of times since, and it often works.

We may seem to have come a long way from relating honesty to happiness as part of its spiritual manifestations, but actually, we've been on the trail, for knowing yourself is a vital step. Now I would like to say a few things about conflict, specifically about saying or pretending one thing and doing the opposite and not even trying to make the two jibe.

This appears when one talks about loving one's enemies but talks eagerly about fighting a war—almost in the same breath. But we don't have to be anything like that extreme to find instances in our daily lives in which our thinking and our talking and pretensions are so contradictory that anyone not accustomed to us would certainly call us insane. Or A-number-one liars.

If you should make a list including fine clothes, liquor, entertainment, jewelry, good health, dogs, a fine house, a boat and the like, and ask a number of people to list them in the order in which they would like to have them, I think you would find health quite near the top of most of the lists. Now if you will investigate the majority of these cases, and not count the time and money each individual spends on doctors and medicines after he is sick, I think you will find that what is actually spent on keeping well compares most unfavorably with amounts spent on many of the other items on the list.

It is true that it is simpler to buy a specific item than it is to preserve our health. For one thing, authorities disagree about what is good for us, and the layman is left in a quandary.

But there are some things that are obvious. Most of us eat too much and too fast; many of us are overweight; some drink too much, sleep too little, and exercise almost not at all. Instead of learning to relax, we take a sleeping pill.

Now (although I wish you would), I am not suggesting

that you start out to take care of your health before you lose it; it is your health and it will be your illness and it is your own business what you do about it. But I do suggest that you get rid of that conflict, that bit of dishonesty with yourself with which you are living. If someone asks you what you want most, admit that it is the new power mower or the new sofa, or the second piece of pie. Of course you would like good health if someone would hand it to you as a gift, but you are willing to work and perhaps even make a sacrifice for some of those other things on the list. So what's wrong with admitting that you actually put good health on the bottom rather than the top, and that you don't want it badly enough to work for it?

You are unwilling to admit this so you change the subject and ask, "What is the point of abolishing conflict?" Well, take the simplest of cases: the inability to make decisions, even in trifles. In my observation, people who can't make up their minds whether to play golf or go swimming, what to have for dinner, which dress or which tie to wear, and so on, will have a disturbed look on their faces. These are infinitesimal conflicts, yet they make for a lack of ease. How much more upsetting must be those bigger conflicts, those discrepancies between pretension and behavior, even when the victim doesn't quite realize he has them! And, for all we know, they may be even harder on us when we don't recognize them.

I guess that many of our other conflicts come under the heading of harboring higher ideals than we have either the ability or the intention to realize. To a certain extent this is desirable; it would be a pity if we couldn't imagine and even aspire to conduct somewhat better than we can achieve. The

trouble is that it usually boils down to our kidding ourselves
and we get our values into a hopeless tangle, while our ideals
are so out of reach that we don't bother to try to do anything
about them.

We need only one example, and first let us ask what are
rules of decent upright behavior supposed to accomplish? I
assume that society doesn't care what we do if we are shut up
in our own room and don't affect anyone but ourselves. So we
will look at some frowned-upon act first from the angle of the
ones whom it affects rather than that of the perpetrator.

A group of friends are having dinner together. You excuse
yourself and go to the room where the women of the party
have left their wraps and handbags. You are broke. You have
to have a dollar, but for some reason you don't want to admit
it, so, instead of asking somebody to lend you one, you help
yourself. Being a considerate person, you take it from the bag
of somebody who can easily spare it and, being a sensible one,
you also see to it that there is enough other money in the
purse so that this dollar will probably not be missed.

You have injured no one. You join the party again, and
there one of the men is making an unpleasant remark to one
of the guests; she is hurt and the others are embarrassed. This
man makes these needlessly upsetting scenes every once in a
while but, all in all, he is a good-natured, likable fellow and it
soon blows over and nobody holds it against him.

But can't you imagine what a hubbub there would be if
somebody had seen you take that dollar? Of the two isolated
acts, which do you think is the more reprehensible? I know
which of the two people I would prefer to have at a party of

mine; I would simply see to it that he didn't go upstairs alone. But there would be nothing I could do to protect my guests from the second offender.

What harm did this thief do to himself? Well, it depends. If he really was a thief, or became one, that would be unfortunate. But if this was merely an emergency and not a habit, if (and this is the important part) he did it without any feeling of guilt, realizing that he was hurting nobody, that the act in itself was inconsequential and was most unlikely to launch him on a career of crime, I can't see that it could do him any harm whatever. The act itself can be called dishonest, but his thinking about it was straight and honest and that seems to me to be the important thing. Whatever it was in him that made it too painful for him to borrow a dollar from someone is, to my mind, more serious than his stealing one.

It all stems from accepting standards that are laid down for us by somebody else. Somewhere along the line society has decided that our dollars are more sacred than our feelings, so the man who may take our money had better not be invited, while the one who merely makes everybody uncomfortable is included. And ponder this: If saying something disagreeable were as socially horrifying as a bit of thievery, the unpleasant people would have long since learned to watch their tongues.

This goes back to the importance of avoiding inner conflicts by straight thinking. To be honest with ourselves about ourselves is a big order indeed; few of us accomplish it and most of us don't know whether we do or not. People whom I consider noticeably dishonest with themselves will say: At least

I'm honest with myself. They think they are and I think I am, but probably I am not, certainly not entirely.

But straight thinking about values, ideals, conduct, and all that long list of things about which we are so mixed up is easier to accomplish. It is interesting to question in our minds every rule of moral and legal and ethical behavior and see if it makes sense. Start with driving a car; the law tells you to drive on the right-hand side of the road. Is that sensible? Well, if you are sensible, you'll do it, even if you don't approve of it. But here is a sign telling you to go twenty-five miles an hour. Ridiculous! So you break that law.

Now take killing. In time of war, it is considered right and even heroic, but if you do it on your own, without the law back of you, you will get into trouble if you're found out. Which is a little puzzling if you haven't been brought up with such a concept.

Speeding, which we accept with a shrug, and murder, which is shocking even when it's legal, are two extremes. The ones in between these, and all of the ethical, moral, and social values that have been established, offer more food for thought and more scope for making our own decisions. For the purpose of achieving personal comfort by abolishing conflict, it makes no difference whether you stick to the old values or make new ones of your own as long as you are honest about it.

In the search for happiness we simply must do some straight thinking, or we're lost. Someone says: "I have often suspected that one of the reasons people keep looking for happiness without getting anywhere is that they don't know exactly what they mean by happiness." That is probably true, and as long as we keep our idea of it vague, overfancy, or too ambitious, or call it a by-product, we won't get very far, I'm afraid.

I have done my best to simplify my meaning, to tell you what I think happiness is, and isn't, and if you agree with me, I think you can go ahead and attain this modest brand if you seriously want to. And I can't conceive of anyone not wanting to be relaxed rather than hectic and tense, peaceful rather than upset, interested instead of bored, gay rather than dull, busy instead of idle. And if, for some obscure reason you are unwilling to work for anything as ordinary as this sounds, why not give it some high-flown title, pursue it tentatively and perhaps become a more desirable person to have around?

VI

Don't Depend on Things That Can Desert You

What, specifically, brings us happiness? We have seen that the five senses, the mind and emotions, and a realm called the spirit all play a part. Now it is time to consider possible sources beyond our own natural endowments—goals and values that are present in our society. Money doesn't bring happiness and, trying hard, could one say anything more trite than that? Sooner or later, everyone you know makes that remark, meaning, presumably, surplus money, enough for luxuries. The poor say it, consoling themselves; the rich say it, knowing what they are talking about. And yet poor and rich alike turn themselves inside out for money, the one trying to get it, the other hanging onto it.

Let's keep in mind that we are talking about luxuries, not necessities and not a reasonable amount of security, and let's make up a little story. There is a man named Sam, and everyone who knows him is aware that he wants a cow more than anything in the world, because he often says that if he could have one wish he'd ask for a cow. Every day, every spare moment, Sam spends digging in the earth, and one neighbor after another asks him why. Sometimes he says it's for a garden, sometimes a cellar, sometimes a well. Since he seems to get little satisfaction out of any of these things his friends are puzzled, and one day one of them asks him why he works so hard and so constantly for things which he doesn't seem to care for much.

"Well, you see," Sam explains, "the only thing I really want is a cow."

"But you won't get one by digging," someone explains to him.

"Oh, I know that," Sam readily agrees, and picks up his spade and goes back to his job.

Obviously poor Sam belongs in a mental institution, along with those who say that what they want most is happiness, admit that surplus money and the luxuries it buys won't give it to them, and at the same time work and work for a finer house and big and little knick-knacks.

Let's look at it another way. You know that material possessions don't bring happiness, but just the same you would give anything to own a car which will give you a chance to show off, even though you don't put it that way. Finally you get one, and there will no doubt be some moments when you will savor the feeling of superiority it gives you.

But you can get just so much pleasure out of an automobile and, since this one has cost you quite a lot of money, it would take a great deal of pleasure to make the expenditure worth it. For the first few nights when you get into bed you may be able to cuddle more happily under the blankets thinking of what is standing in your garage, but that probably won't last a week; a little later it may even be unwise to think about it when you want to go to sleep, if the next payment on it is about due or if the miserable thing keeps getting out of order. And if the coffee is too hot at breakfast when you're in a hurry to make your train, if your wife says *once more*, damn it, that the living-room rug is a disgrace, if your boss jumps on you for something your idiot of a secretary neglected to do, if you suspect you have ulcers but are afraid to go to your doctor to find out, how does your fine car help you to take all this non-chalantly? The sad fact is that any material possession may bring isolated moments of satisfaction, but it will do nothing whatever to help you to face and control the many trifles which make up your day and your life. If a pleasant glow inside, a relaxed feeling, is what we have decided to call happiness, ask yourself how many hours a month of this desired commodity you can hope to get out of your new car. Not many, and you may even find you're in the red as far as peace is concerned.

One drawback to material possessions is that there are so awfully many of them. You have fifty and now you want fifty-one; there's no end to it. Well, who wants to just sit like a lump and be satisfied? What's wrong with striving? Nothing, and if I were five years old I wouldn't be ashamed to say: I have a doll and now I want a cradle for her and a set of dishes. But after I reached forty I hope I would be hesitant about admitting that I was spending much time working for, or wishing for, unnecessary material possessions. With forty years in which to assemble some values, I would hope to have done better than that.

However, this attitude needs some explaining and toning down. In a previous chapter I had quite a bit to say about the pleasure we can get through our five senses. Buying a new record, a rosebush, a bottle of perfume, a car teeming with gadgets means spending money for a luxury, and what's wrong with that? Nothing, providing we are getting our money's worth of enjoyment, providing we expect these things to do only so much for us and no more.

Let's take a look at this in terms of negative and positive pleasure. A large part of the purchase of superfluities is probably an effort to get rid of an unpleasant feeling rather than to buy a pleasant one. For instance, the faded rug, outmoded car, unfashionable dress may annoy us, not for aesthetic reasons but social ones. If the old rug was a valuable antique you would cherish it; then age would be a virtue. You liked the car, the dress, a year or so ago and they haven't changed appreciably. You don't get tired of your engagement ring and throw it away.

Shortly after I wrote that last sentence I read in one of Vance Packard's books that some of you do. He says that women are getting rid of their engagement rings and buying new ones. If I knew that a majority of the women who can afford to do that were actually doing it, I think I would throw this manuscript into the fire, for if people's values have become that foreign to me, I am wasting my time. But I am a confirmed optimist and, although I know that snobbish values abound, I simply can't believe that many of you go as far as that.

But even an optimist knows to some extent what is going on. All your old things disturb you, and as fast as you can you buy new ones to get rid of the disturbance—a negative reason. This wouldn't be so deplorable if now you spent your time enjoying the things you bought at a sacrifice of time, energy, money. But you don't; sadly enough, instead of thinking of these fine new possessions, now you put your mind on acquiring something else. It's a vicious circle, and it can go on until the day you die if you don't grow up and sort out your values.

To what extent will good health support us in our pursuit of happiness? It helps, certainly, and if we include mental health in our concept it will give us an excellent start. It is a good, firm foundation, but is not, of course, a synonym for peace, serenity, pleasure. No matter what our objective, however, we will get farther if we have good health, from a child starting in kindergarten to a ninety-year-old, whose sole aim now is to reach ninety-one.

But let us not mistake either health or a bland, so-called "normality" for happiness. I know of no one who gets more out of living than a friend of ours who has poor health, works hard for the bare necessities, and has a persecution complex.

He lives in a cold-water flat in New York, has an all-night job, and enjoys life almost every waking moment. Except for the feeling that this one and that one is out to do him harm, he has a good mind and thinks clearly. He spends his leisure time painting, reading, and walking in the park or along the street or through a store, missing nothing, pleased with everything.

He told me that once he went into a ten-cent store and saw on a counter a lot of little bells which he liked; he thought his cat would enjoy them, too, and they cost so little he decided to buy one.

"But I didn't," he said. "I couldn't for they had the most delightful tinkle; first I'd try one and then another and I simply couldn't make up my mind which sound was the loveliest."

Now do I hear you saying: Oh, sure, some crazy people are happy, but who wants to be crazy? Perhaps he is a little insane, but is it any more abnormal for an adult to be extravagantly delighted with the tinkling of a bell than it is to go all to pieces over the dripping of a faucet?

One more thing about my friend that is unusual but I don't think abnormal: Our train service to New York is poor; the alternative is a bus, but for some reason most of the people we know avoid that and, through the thirty years that we've lived here, I doubt if a dozen people have come or left by bus. This man had no such prejudice, and once we got a four-page letter from him, describing his trip back to New York. He had enjoyed literally hundreds of things that most of us never see. His letter wasn't childish and wasn't crazy; it was poetic and beautiful and if only I had saved it, I would share it with you.

Is leisure happiness? Like money and health it can help, but all we need do is look at the lonely old people with time hanging heavy on their hands, to know that it, alone, doesn't do the trick. I almost believe (and please don't jump down my throat) that it's better, when you get old, to be a little sick and poor than to be alone with health and money and to have lived in such a way that your days are now empty. The former at least have something to be concerned about; what can the latter wish for? What hope is there? The sick can take another pill and hope that it will make them feel better; the poor can count the pennies and make a decision: mend the old gloves once more and maybe buy a new hairbrush. But those others, what *alive* thing can they think about?

Plenty, of course, if they have learned to put happiness into their hours instead of empty activity. Recently an intelligent friend of mine, a man in his early forties, said that people had gone crazy over shorter hours and when they got all that time off they didn't know what to do with it. I didn't have to ask him what he did with his, for I knew. He plays golf in season, and out of season he counts the days until he will be able to play it again. The trouble with that is that during the winter he is restless and often short-tempered and doesn't know what to do with his free time. While he is enjoying himself playing golf he seems like a happy person, but he has put all his eggs in one basket, and we specified balanced enjoyment.

Most of the young women I know, especially those with children, want leisure desperately and are sure that when they get it it will spell happiness for them; they want to get away from the hectic business of having so many demands made on their time. But watch them if they get some of this longed-for leisure; if possible, their days become more hectic than ever. Their minds are full of all the things they resented not being able to do, and they often begin cramming all these activities into their insufficient newly found free time and soon are spinning even faster than before. Leisure, the privilege of choosing what to do with our time, may give us nothing at all; it can even be a menace.

Hand in hand with free time comes that good old stand-by, the hobby. Again, this helps toward filling our hours pleasantly; presumably a hobby is some kind of work or activity which we enjoy, which we pursue because we want to, rather than because we must. It would therefore seem a bit ironic if we didn't have a good time doing it.

Let's not confuse enjoyment of a hobby with happiness, however, not even with the rather modest variety we are trying here to learn how to attain. A hobby can be almost worthless if you have retired and have adopted it only to fill your empty hours. It then may become a merely better-than-nothing affair, may bore you or make you irritable. Or you may take up something which completely fascinates you, uses up more of your time than you intended it should, and thus deprives your wife of enjoying the freedom from various chores which she thought she would have, now that you are retired. Perhaps you think she is unreasonable; why shouldn't she continue to hold up her end of it? Nothing has changed as far as she is concerned; you are still "supporting" her. Or perhaps the trouble is that you become so involved in your activities that you are late to meals, are unsociable, absent-minded, and, again, irritable, this time not because you are bored, but tired. Your wife, who never nagged formerly, may begin to, now that you are more or less underfoot.

Well, I'm making up all sorts of things that may never happen to you, but I hope I've made my point: a hobby is merely an activity, a side issue, usually a desirable one, and can be one of the many things that help us to achieve happiness, but is by no means sufficient in itself.

And now comes the opposite of leisure and a hobby: the work we do, not because we want to but because we must. You may be surprised that I give this rather a high rating. We may grumble about it, we may believe that our lives would be far pleasanter if we weren't obliged to work, but I think we are mistaken. Often even a job that we thoroughly dislike will, in a negative way and to some extent, keep us from wallowing in our misery.

Let's have a quick look at those unfortunate people who aren't obliged to do anything. Beginning with the children, I am convinced that they would be much happier if they were taught while still very young that there were certain jobs they must do. And they should, of course, be made to feel that their work is a helpful, even necessary, contribution.

As far back as I can remember, each one of us nine children had his separate and allotted tasks. There was no bickering about who would do what; it would have seemed as absurd for two of us to argue about which one should wash the dishes and which fill the lamps with kerosene as it would have been if Dad and Mother had argued about which one should get in the buggy and go to visit schools (Dad was County Superintendent) and which one stay at home and get the meals. If it was your job to fill the lamps you did it without being told to, and I wouldn't be surprised if Mother was even capable of giving you the feeling, without saying a word, that we would all sit around all evening in darkness but for you.

On a Kansas farm, sixty or seventy years ago, it must have been easy enough to think up jobs for nine children; in a modern apartment, or even a suburban home, I suppose it takes some doing to convince even two or three that they are needed. Girls are easier to find work for than boys, for they can be made to sew, dust, cook. When we are far enough advanced to get over the fanciful notion that some jobs aren't "suitable" for boys, we'll be better off. I have a friend who went to Russia some thirty years ago, and he came back with this story: he was surprised at how many of the doctors were women and he asked one of the male physicians if women made as good doctors as men. The physician didn't understand the question. After a good deal of explaining back and forth, it turned out that such a question had no more meaning for him than if my friend had asked if men who wore mustaches were better doctors than those who didn't. What on earth did a mustache—or sex—have to do with the study of medicine?

There has been so much talk in recent years of those poor devils who retire while they are still able to work and are lost, with time hanging heavily on their hands, that we can skip them, just taking everybody's word for it that they are miserable. And we have already covered those old people who still could do some work if only they were obliged to, but who can't fill their hours with any kind of satisfying activity just for the sake of keeping in motion.

What about the idle rich, those who have never in a long life had to do any work for the purpose of making a living? There are relatively few of these, so we can dispose of them quickly, sorry as we may be for them. To me they are like people who sit through a play, enjoying it superficially but entirely missing the point. They go through life without any real conception of what is going on basically in the lives of all the millions who are forced to do something in order to stay alive. They are not a part of the stream of life, merely onlookers, sitting on the bank.

And now for the workers. Instead of trying to convince you that you should be thankful that you have to work, I'm going to tell you how I feel about it. I like to know, when I get up each morning, that there are jobs which I must do. When I open my eyes to a new day, I would hate to have to say to myself over and over again: It makes no practical difference to me or to anyone else whether I get up or not. No job will be left undone if I lie here all day. I have no obligation that is important to anybody, that I can't easily skip if I want to. The adjective that best describes me is "superfluous."

Please don't tell me that one can fill one's life with obligations if one wants to; it is the having to that counts. Voluntary tasks are short-term obligations; you can sign off as soon as you are no longer in the mood, but you can't suddenly decide to stop making a living if you need to in order to eat.

I've had some experience with the brand of obligation that is optional. People whose time is their own promise to come in one day a week, or perhaps three afternoons a week, to help with some big mailing job, let us say, for some cause they believe in. Now they don't show up at all; again, they run in for an hour and run out again. In my experience the voluntary workers in any project who are worth their salt are those who have to earn a living, who make their contributions in the evening after work and usually overdo it. This doesn't necessarily mean that they are more unselfish than the idle rich; it may mean only that they realize that if there is a job to be done somebody actually has to do some work. Also, the idlers are being constantly interrupted in their voluntary commitments; if they feel like taking a trip around the world, why should a mere job of work interfere?

Since I wrote that last paragraph I came into contact with two hospitals, one in Long Island and one in Ridgewood, New Jersey, and was impressed with the number, efficiency, and faithfulness of their volunteer workers. I don't take back what I said about this kind of worker in general, but I want to say that I realize there are exceptions.

Luckily, most of us must work; unluckily, many of us dislike it. I like every kind of work except cleaning the oven and the bathtub; hard as I try, I just haven't learned to enjoy those two jobs. But I know exactly why I like to work and I believe that anyone who wants to can learn the trick, and since you are probably going to spend a lot of time working, I should think you'd prefer to like it. The formula couldn't be simpler: keep your mind on what you're doing. If you are the kind of woman who turns on the radio while you do your housework, however, and by this means manage not to mind whatever job you're at, you need no suggestions from me. But if your work is out of doors or away from home, you can't use this handy

device. I think you may be surprised—and gratified—to discover how unobnoxious any task or occupation is when you
give it your full attention and take an interest in doing it as
well as you can.

I am glad that I have had to work for a living all of my
adult life, but of course that in itself won't find happiness for
anybody. It can even tell against us if we allow it to.

How about "Be good and you'll be happy"? First of all,
being human, who can be really good? Second, who wants to
be while everybody else is just so-so? Third, what is "good"?
Most of us try to be decent, fairly honest, fairly reliable, and so
on through the various virtues, but in order to be what might
be considered thoroughly good I suppose we would have to be
selfless, and I should think that that might make selfish and
spoiled people out of those with whom we are closely associ-
ated, which seems unfair to them. Don't they, too, have a
right to be good and happy?

If you are going to make a project of being good, don't you
have to love everybody? Do you think you could possibly
swing that? And what are you going to do about giving? I
should think that the good person would feel impelled to give
generously of everything he had, including himself, but how
about this business of its being more blessed to give than to
receive? Is he going to resign himself to taking, rather than
giving, or is he going to insist on having the more blessed end
of it? It seems to me that rather than setting out to be good
in a big way, we would do better to work on some of the less
inclusive aims which, if achieved, will add up to a modest
brand of goodness with the added advantage of giving us a

measure of inner peace. We could try to be understanding, compassionate, uncritical, relaxed, unhurried, and that is no small order.

I have noticed one characteristic of those people who set out to be good, noble, unselfish. They cannot, unfortunately, be as perfect as they want to be, and therefore feel guilty and become upset when they fall short of their impossible standard and are prone to be oversensitive to criticism. If I could choose, I think I would prefer to live with an inconsiderate person than one who was consciously, elaborately considerate. I believe I could think up some way to cope with the former, but I've had some small experience with the latter and have found them almost impossible to handle.

Running hand in hand with the "good" people are those who are full of good deeds, either doing things for individuals or working for some cause. This may help them to forget themselves part of the time, but that in itself is an extremely negative substitute for happiness.

What about an attractive appearance? It embarrasses me a little to even suggest that anyone could think that this is a real guarantee of happiness, yet when you consider the money some men will spend on a suit of clothes and the millions spent in beauty parlors, on cosmetics, jewelry, fur coats, and rather awful dresses because they're in style, people must expect a good deal from merely their outward appearance. And I have to admit that we do get something from a bath, some strokes of the hairbrush, a dab of powder and perfume and lipstick, a becoming dress. They all can boost the morale, but please, let's not be too puerile; let's not expect them to bring us happiness.

We've already had a glance at that good old medicine the doctor orders when we get all tied up in knots: a vacation, a trip, a change of scene. It usually helps a little, momentarily, the unfortunate part being that we have to take ourselves with us, and it's ourselves, not the geography, who are all awry. The trip will probably do us some good, temporarily, and so may phenobarbital, temporarily, but it solves no problems.

Let's have a look at fame; surely one can squeeze some happiness out of prestige? Not world fame; few of us will reach that, but what's wrong with the local variety? What about getting the prize oftener than anyone else in the club for your splendid flower arrangements? Or topping everyone at golf?

The question arises: which would you rather be, liked or envied? Some people can manage to be popular in spite of walking off with all the prizes, but it takes some doing. When one of my older sisters was in her late teens and early twenties she was the most popular girl in her crowd, and I don't want to belittle her appeal, but perhaps part of it was because she never entered any sort of contest without walking off with the booby prize. And she didn't mind a bit.

We hang onto our tiny bit of fame as a miser hoards his money. And this I'll tell you, my friends and foes: the miser has a better chance of keeping his money than we have of holding onto our fame, and also he is less likely to bore his friends with it. What's more, don't imagine that it's only the little people who behave like this; I know a few specimens whose renown is much wider, and they are just as nervous about it as the little frogs.

Fame definitely doesn't bring serenity, and you definitely can't trust it not to desert you. Much better to get yourself an oxalis plant; you can enjoy it without boring anybody, and if it should die you can buy another.

What about power? Can one achieve, or even want, power without being greedy? A glutton, whether the end he has in view is food, money, admiration, or whatever, is quite un- lovely, but the thirst to dominate, to control, surely makes a monstrosity out of a person. Here I may get in beyond my depth, for a fine distinction must be made between leadership for a presumably worthy purpose and a craving for power merely to quench the thirst for it. (In passing, I suppose it's accurate to add that the thirst is never satisfied.) There is a distinction between controlling one's children and dominating one's husband or wife; the first is a job, the other is a disease.

How about friends, family, human relations? We all know that our contacts with other people can be inspiring, merely pleasant, painful, dull, and we will go into this further when we discuss love.

Let's have a look at sex; the confusion in our thinking about this and love is abysmal. A physical attraction is mistaken for love, and marriage often follows, then disillusion. How are young people to know which is which?

Sex has played a peculiar role in our literature. When I was growing up, it certainly wasn't mentioned, as such, between any two normal people who were going to get married and live happily ever after. And if a girl "slipped," that was the end of her. Then sex reared its unmentionable head in books; D. H. Lawrence's *Lady Chatterley's Lover* fairly reeks with it, and when I read that book I became as bored with the constantly repeated description of the physical act, as I would have if the author had gone on, page after page, with endless descriptions of two people eating together—chewing, swallowing, chewing again.

But at least Lawrence's lovers were acquainted with each other, and, dull as the book is, it isn't quite as ridiculous as the modern novels (detective and otherwise) in which girls and men fall into each others' arms within a few seconds after they first meet. In many current novels a woman can't enter the scene without mention of her anatomy, and not once but almost every time she moves or speaks; I, for one, am so sick of women's breasts that I wish they didn't exist.

The modern idea is to tell our children the facts of life, and that is probably more sensible than the way we were brought up—in complete ignorance. However, this new attitude hasn't gone on long enough for the parents to be casual about it; their diffident attitude is sensed, I believe, by the child, and it will have to change before the sex act is put in its proper perspective.

I suppose the publishers of books have a fairly good idea of what sells, and as long as our literature reeks of sex (the physical act, that is, without love), it must mean that we are still contaminated with the old-fashioned attitude of sex being a forbidden and therefore fascinating subject. And as long as that feeling persists, no matter how we explain it to our children, they are going to snicker about it and feel pleasantly wicked when they come across it in books or on the screen—or in their own experimentations.

Anyone who claims that sex makes for happiness means, I suppose, when it is combined with love, for without that we must simply recognize it as a brief physical pleasure, and include its sensations along with those of the five senses. Since in the realm of prostitution, the act is often performed with a complete and sometimes a rather unappealing stranger, paid for with a few dollars and then forgotten, it is odd indeed that it is this same act that constitutes being "untrue" to one's husband or wife. My husband can sit around adoring some other woman, but as long as he doesn't have sexual intercourse with her he is "true" to me. It is most baffling, all this, and, until we go forward a little in our thinking, sex will continue to be the cause of a great deal of unhappiness as well as happiness. Love is, of course, another matter, and one we will come to in due course.

And now we must consider religion as a possible source of happiness. Even if I could prove that religion gives us inner peace (which I should think we would have a right to expect), it wouldn't help you at all, for if you are a religious person and it does give you this peace, you don't need any help, and if you aren't religious, there is no way that I know of to voluntarily become so. Religion is a matter of faith; you have it or you don't, and I don't believe that any amount of wishing for it, of studying or striving to attain it, will get you anywhere.

But what about all these religious people who go to church, who believe in a God and a hereafter, and yet, by and large, seem neither better nor happier than those who don't? Is that satisfactory? Do the former expect to be so happy when they get to Heaven and for the rest of eternity that they can't be bothered to feel good for the relatively short time they are obliged to spend on this earth? But if that is true, why aren't they eager to go? The religious people I know don't seem in any more of a hurry to die than the irreligious ones, even when they aren't having a very good time here.

Religion does seem to fortify many people in times of stress, yet we have already taken note of the fact that, in times of great trouble and sorrow, most of us gather together our resources and behave courageously and even feel a certain inner strength. What we need is something to lean on and lead us when a wife scolds, a husband complains about the roast, the children get out of hand, the boss barks unreasonably or even with reason. I don't believe that religious people face these trials a bit more cheerily than do the unbelievers; neither have I noticed that their values are loftier or even saner. You might be excused for thinking that a man who was looking forward to being happy through eternity would find it almost impossible to care what kind of a car he rode in in the meantime, or that his churchgoing wife would mind that her clothes were out of style. Or, assuming that a religious person hadn't behaved as well as he felt he should and was slightly nervous about his chances of going straight to Heaven, wouldn't you think he would be so busy reforming that he wouldn't have time to notice cars or styles? Here is one thing that I should think might make some people awfully nervous: what if they got to Heaven and found that the angel sitting next to them playing a harp was a Negro or a Jew?

Here is a little story about my grandfather who, as I have said, was a thoroughly good man and a deeply religious one. His wife, who incidentally didn't have a Quaker background, was a nagger of the first magnitude. She could, and did, go on and on about nothing. I never heard my grandfather answer back, which probably irritated her all the more. Nor did I ever even see a look on his face that said he would love to slap her. (There is a story about an old Quaker who had a wife like that, and every now and then he would say to her, "I don't heed thee any more than I heed the wind a-blowing.") But back to my grandfather: my father's sister told us that Grandpa Stout would notice Grandma's nagging—oh, perhaps once a month or so—and when he did, he would just quietly but firmly say, "Sophie, thee has said enough." And, so Aunt Mary told us, Sophie kept still then for the rest of the day.

The trouble with that story in connection with religion is that it is no proof that it was Grandpa's religion that gave him immunity from the pettiness around him. It could have been his temperament, or life may have taught him how to be serene, no matter what. One example isn't enough; before we can be sure that religion brings happiness we have to see that the great majority of religious people are happier, week in and week out and all day long, than the majority of agnostics and infidels. In my observation, this isn't so, and therefore I must conclude that religion, like all the rest of the list we've gone through, brings us many happy moments but in most cases can't be relied on through thick and thin.

I have saved the most promising to the last: love. And having saved it, I find it disappointing. Surely there is no more misused, more misunderstood word in any language; it is used to include our attitude toward food, animals, music, scenery, reading—there are far too many to enumerate. Then comes love for humans, which may range from a more or less brief physical attraction to a devotion that lasts a lifetime. There is love of country, which may be raised to such a high level (or sunk to such a low one) that we will rush forth to kill our fellow creatures for its sake. And there is love of God, of humanity in the large, and love of life.

With that wide conception it is just plain silly to pretend to cover it unless you write a whole book about it. Even cutting it down to include only individual human beings, the word is still used indiscriminately enough to water down its meaning to almost nothing. Letters to people whom we care for only casually nowadays are signed "Love." Eager to make some distinction between these and the ones we really care for, we are sometimes driven to end a letter "With all my love," which is certainly an overstatement.

Let's abandon love for a moment and have a look at the people we merely like. We have already decided that we feel better when we're thinking about someone we like than someone we don't, and of course liking people does help. But how about when we are with them? I find it easy enough to like a bore but can I help it if I don't enjoy him? As a matter of fact, I actually dislike very few people and am totally indifferent to none, which means that I like practically everybody I know, but enjoying them is quite another story. I must conclude, then, that merely liking people doesn't in itself add measurably to my happiness, although it certainly soft-pedals my discomfort.

I don't think that being loved (a passive thing) adds much to one's happiness, pleasant as it is, and of course it is true that an unrequited love can make one miserable. There is no doubt that we get both pain and pleasure out of loving, and if jealousy accompanies it, it can be hell. If the loved one is ill or in trouble or unkind to us, we suffer. If our children disappoint us, we agonize. If we let our love be smeared with bickerings, it is ugly. We can get a great deal of joy out of loving and being loved, but it has its ups and downs and is something that can be lost. And here we are searching for a brand of happiness that we can hang onto, no matter what.

I haven't begun to cover this endless subject but I don't believe it can be constructively pursued by itself, without relation to other factors. For we can't force ourselves to love and cannot make anyone love us. You must have seen people trying desperately to buy affection with gifts, with good deeds. It can't be done. As for liking and loving others, we can try to be uncritical, understanding, compassionate, and this may help a little toward liking more people, just as it may also help others to like us.

Loving life may be one road to happiness, possibly even synonymous with it, but how to achieve it? It's a big order, so let's break it down into something we can grasp. A person's life is made up of years, months, weeks, days, and hours, and instead of trying to love all of it, all of a sudden, when we haven't given the idea much thought (and perhaps don't even like our lives very much), how about taking it hour by hour?

If, by conscious effort, we can make one hour a pleasant one (and surely we can accomplish that), we have made a start. Then, before we know it, we will often have a whole enjoyable day. Then weeks, then months, then years, and, almost without realizing how it happened, we will wake up each morning with pleasant thoughts and a zest for living. And if this feeling stands by us all day long, I see nothing against calling it happiness.

VII

Making Mountains Out of Molehills

Whoever thought up human beings, with all their good and bad potentialities, was most ingenious in figuring out ways to make them suffer needlessly. Perhaps "suffer" is too strong a word for the sort of thing I have in mind, but it may be that the countless insignificant daily annoyances and trifling upsets take more out of us in the long run than a man-sized job of legitimate agony, which we undergo much less frequently. We have already noted that it isn't unusual to face a great sorrow with courage and dignity, but it is unfortunately most common to handle small irritations with infantile ineptness.

Most of us, if we decide to make an honest attempt to

achieve some measure of happiness, will have to resign ourselves to entering the primer class. In the matter of learning
how to live a more satisfying life, you start with a handicap
which a child doesn't have, because there are a great many
things that you must unlearn, many habits that you must dis-
card.

So now when I suggest that you actually punish yourself
when you fail in some small endeavor, I am doing it in all
seriousness. In this undertaking you have no teacher to see to
it that you toe the mark, and if you backslide too often you
may become discouraged and abandon the whole business,
which would be a pity. If you are a mere infant in the pursuit
of happiness, there is nothing humiliating or ridiculous in
treating yourself as one.

First I am going to tell a story that has nothing to do with
being happy, but it illustrates the sort of procedure I have in
mind. A friend of ours was sure that she was smoking too
much and tried to cut down or quit, and had no luck doing
either. Finally she appealed to me; surely, she said, I could
think up something that would work. I told her I would have
to take a little time and think about it; she had already tried
many tricks which hadn't helped, such as having her husband
take all the cigarettes with him when he left for work in the
morning.

A day or so later I telephoned her with the news that I had
thought up something that would work if she could go through
with it. And you should know this about her: her husband
had a good job, they had five children, they didn't have to

worry unduly about money but neither did they have any to throw around.

I told her this: Buy a package of cigarettes and also have a ten-dollar bill changed into quarters. Put all this in a box and keep an empty box sitting by it. Every time you smoke one of the cigarettes put a quarter into the second box. When the quarters are all transferred put them back into the first box (in which you will put more cigarettes as you run out), but at this point you must give me a ten-dollar bill. And I can see by the gleam in your eyes that you think that will be a slick way to make you save money but it doesn't work like that, for that wouldn't help you to stop smoking. You won't get the bill back; I'll give it to some cause and to one you don't believe in.

In short, every time she smoked a cigarette she punished herself not only by losing a quarter but, worse, by helping out some activity of which she disapproved. It took her several months to make up her mind to attempt anything so drastic, for she couldn't afford to waste much money and she knew what a hold smoking had on her. However, her concern over what it might be doing to her health and her feeling of obligation to the five children she had brought into the world finally won the day; she undertook the project and won the battle. She is convinced that she never could have done it by will power alone. Knowing that she must transfer a quarter every time she smoked a cigarette, she would often start to light one and then stop and decide to wait another fifteen minutes, another hour. She did some suffering and so did I, for she and I have about the same values and it was painful to me to hand out ten-dollar bills to something I didn't believe in either.

I have heard that "they" have concluded that smoking has a physiological hold on the addict, and therefore I suppose it is a more stubborn and difficult habit to deal with than most of the kind I am trying to persuade you to abandon. Start with one that is relatively easy to cure; let's say that when you knock the ashes out of your pipe you almost invariably spill some and this annoys your wife and she complains. Obviously, it's unreasonable for her to be unpleasant about such a trifle, but you are going to change yourself, not her, remember. So since this habit of yours causes some friction, you decide to cure it, and since you don't especially enjoy spilling ashes, the only trick here is to remember to be careful. That's not as easy as it sounds, since we all go about doing things with our minds on something else. But let's say that the pipe of the day you enjoy most is that one after dinner when you settle down with a book, so, from now on, every time you spill ashes you punish yourself by omitting that pipe the following evening. My guess is that it will be no time at all before you remember not to spill. And do you know what? If in some tender, or joking, or even offhand way you let your wife know that you are making this effort to please her, she *will* be pleased and touched and perhaps even say, "Dear, what do I care? It isn't important," ignoring the fact that she has been making herself a little obnoxious about it.

But what if you are this tidy wife; your husband hasn't decided to try to take the little disturbances out of your mutual relations, but you have. If there is one thing you simply can't endure, it is spilled ashes, and that man you married (and still love, although sometimes you wonder how you manage to keep on, with him being so careless and inconsiderate) knows perfectly well that it gets you down when he is so sloppy with ashes, for you invariably snap at him when he does it, and you don't like to snap. Sometimes he grunts or gives you a dis-gusted look, and once in a while he gets impatient. Then you both mildly hate each other for a little while, and you clean up the mess with a martyred look on your face.

It should be obvious to anyone that he is in the wrong, for any grown man who hasn't palsy should be able to knock a few ashes out of a pipe without spilling. For years you've tried to cure him of this careless habit, getting nowhere. But now you have a new objective; you've undertaken to establish a pleasant atmosphere around you, so, since you apparently can't cure your husband of a habit that annoys you, the only alterna-tive is to cure yourself of minding it.

First you may try will power and find it doesn't work. You are a neat person (possibly too much so for your own com-fort and that of those who have to live with you) and you can tell yourself a thousand times that you don't mind spilled ashes, but you do mind. However, with determination you can at least keep still about them and that's fine for the guilty party (your husband), but this project isn't for him; it is serenity for yourself that you are seeking. So the necessary step is to learn not to mind the spilling, and here, I believe, a simple little punishment may achieve your purpose: when your hus-band spills ashes let them lie there the rest of the evening and all the next day and right up until the regular cleaning day comes around. Not to punish him, of course, for he probably won't care and may not even notice them. But since you are a meticulous person the sight of these ashes will drive you crazy, and you are likely to find that the immediate cleaning up, over and over, of spilled ashes becomes a pleasure compared to what you're going through. A possible by-product of this (although you had better not count on it) is that your husband may notice that you no longer scold when he spills and that after all you aren't the waspish old fusser that he was beginning to fear he had married, and he may even be so appreciative that he'll be a little more careful. But you no longer care if he isn't, don't forget that.

If you are bored with all this and think what a waste of time it is for me to go on and on about an infinitesimal trifle, just watch yourself and the people around you for a few days. Choose some person you are near all day, either at home or in the office, and keep count of all the negative and unpleasant things which make up his day. The rush, the tension, the critical remarks, the irritable tone of voice, the petty arguments, perhaps temper. And probably every one of these ugly happenings is a trifle which will have no importance to him by tomorrow.

I said something like this to a friend who dropped in recently. He had had a minor operation, and from the hospital had gone to an aunt's home to recuperate. He told me, most feelingly, that she had driven him nearly out of his mind, discussing from breakfast until lunchtime what they should have for lunch, and from then on what she was planning for dinner. He was pointing out that his aunt was allowing unimportant trifles to clog her day, not even noticing that he was revealing the fact that his irritation was out of order, too. Admittedly he had allowed his aunt's fussiness to disturb him to such an extent that it had delayed his recovery. It is true he had nothing to do but sit and listen, which was unfortunate, but even while we are busy, running along with our activities, like an accompaniment to a song, are words, thoughts, emotions, and perceptions, and it is the quality of this accompaniment that sets the tone of our existence. And, I am sorry to say, this tone is in large measure so negative and petty that, if one wants to try to put some beauty and life into it, one has to consider things as trifling as getting upset over spilled ashes or a talkative aunt.

Now I am going to pay you the compliment of assuming that you can take this punishment trick from here and work it out without my help. As I did, choose an easy one to start with, so that you will be sure to succeed; this will give you courage to go on. You will need it, and will power and determination; above all, you must want serenity earnestly enough to make an effort to get it. And always keep this in mind: you aren't working to improve your behavior but toward improving the way you feel inside. That's all that matters, basically.

There are qualities which are desirable as such but which we mishandle. A sense of justice is an excellent commodity, but if we ourselves are involved we are often inclined to be swayed by our own interests. We can also wear ourselves out to no good purpose bursting with righteous indignation even when we aren't personally involved and have neither the intention nor the power to do anything toward righting the wrong.

I don't believe I ever heard my mother express indignation. But she had a healthy sense of justice and acted accordingly, even when it was to her disadvantage to do so. She once got hurt when she was getting off a streetcar, and the conductor took her name and address and an adjuster called on her and offered her a few hundred dollars to settle any claim she intended to make. It was more than ample, for she wasn't badly hurt.

Mother said, "You don't owe me anything; it was my own carelessness."

The poor fellow begged her to take some money and sign on the dotted line, for he naturally thought that she intended to sue. He couldn't understand a person whose sense of justice worked both ways.

Standing up for our rights in our relations with others is at the bottom of a tremendous amount of unnecessary unpleasantness and an awful lot of work besides. It is particularly active among people who live together, as we have seen with regard to husbands and wives. Few grownup, intelligent, and reasonably sensitive people will go into battle with each other when they have company, but if you watch for it (and often it is so apparent that you don't have to watch) you can spot the particular little duties which the wife or husband feels belong to the other one but which just now are being shoved off onto him. It is his job, say, or his turn to clear away the dishes and bring in the dessert, but he is engrossed (probably purposely, she thinks) in a long story to his dinner partner. Or vice versa. This makes for some tension, even a remark, and possibly a snappish one.

On one such occasion the situation promised to develop into an open and aboveboard argument. There were ten of us; the host and hostess were in their sixties (time enough to learn a value or two) and on the whole they were sensible, tactful, and intelligent. Well, clearing away the dishes for ten people does amount to quite a job, and the question arose of whose turn it was to remove them. When it got to the point of his stubborn determination not to be imposed on, the host said in a voice which indicated that he meant to be adamant:

"Well, I know absolutely that I took them out the last time."

Before the hostess had time to answer (and she appeared to be going to, to some purpose) somebody said to her husband, "Then how much more wonderful of you it will be if you take them out now."

It got a laugh, even from the host, and he took care of the dishes. I consider this to have been an inspired remark, not on account of the laugh it got but because the situation was neatly saved and embarrassment avoided.

Childish of them? Yes, but not quite as much so as it seems on the face of it, because of course neither minded the work involved; that flaming sense of justice had reared its ridiculous head. There are probably at least a thousand ways in which we could manage to feel imposed on, if we gave the matter some good constructive thought—or no thought at all, letting our emotions take over.

There is that momentous matter of which one should do the carving. I can remember the time when the question never arose; it was the man's job. But in recent years the men seem to be trying to shove it off onto the women, who, whether they like to carve or not, have no intention of being exploited.

In our household I always did the carving. Fred hated to, and I didn't care one way or the other and don't even mind that I'm not very good at it. But after thirty years of it I at last became fed up with the conversation which all too often accompanied my performance, if there were guests who knew us well enough to get personal. First there would be some indignation at Fred from the women, because he "made" me carve. When I answered that I didn't mind, they replied that that wasn't the point; it was the man's job. And then, for fear their husbands were noticing what an angel I was, doing a man's job without complaining, they called attention to how badly I was doing it. Here they had something, but Fred would come to my defense, saying that he couldn't do any better. Someone would say, nonsense, anyone who could carve (as he had, out of wood) that beautiful horse there on the mantel could certainly cut up a leg of lamb without hacking it to bits.

Bored with all this one morning, after the guests of the previous evening had gone to extremes with their "the-man-should-carve-and-just-see-how-badly-Ruth-does-it" routine, I summoned my gray cells and put them to work. In any case it was inefficient to do the carving at the table, for everybody's food got cold while I performed. So now I carve in the kitchen, put the meat on a platter, and keep it warm in the oven while I do the last-minute jobs, even though the roast dries out a little.

One way to avoid feeling that you are unfairly treated is by not letting the wrongdoer know your preferences. Find out his and how strongly he feels about them, and conduct yourself accordingly.

On the whole, it is well to disabuse yourself of the notion that certain things are a man's job and others a woman's. It will probably be difficult for you to decide that you should darn your own socks and sew on your own buttons, even if your wife also goes to a job each day or if there are so many children that she is busier than you are. And you probably won't have to sink that low, for it isn't likely to have occurred to her either that a man is as able as a woman to wield a needle. But there are any number of tasks to which sex clings without any justification; if possible, get rid of the notion that they are either beyond you or beneath you.

You might even be ashamed of this second attitude if I can persuade you that you are, in this respect, thinking and behaving like an ignorant and unintelligent woman whose young daughter came to help me with the housework many years ago. Fred was in bed with a badly infected toe, and I had to get up several times during the night to change the dressing. I'm fairly worthless when I don't get enough sleep, and I found that being nurse, housekeeper, cook, along with a vast unwillingness to let my vegetable garden be taken over by weeds (this was before I had learned that one needn't have any weeds) was too much for me.

This girl of about sixteen came to give me a hand. I don't find it easy to tell other people what to do, and also, I'm sorry to say, she didn't seem to be the type who could do much of anything without supervision after I had told her. So I asked her which she preferred: should we do the housework together and then both go out to the vegetable patch and work there, or would she rather do the housework alone? She chose the former and we got along splendidly.

Her brother drove her to the house each morning and called for her in the late afternoon. On the third day when he came to get his sister, his mother came with him; she wanted the pay that was due, saying that her daughter was not coming back to work for a woman who treated her like a common farm hand, making her go out into the field and hoe corn, of all unheard-of insults!

I was flabbergasted; I knew there was no use to try to explain that I had given the girl a choice, and that I considered hoeing corn as upright and honorable (and not harder to do and even pleasanter) as sweeping a floor or making a bed. In fact, if you want to go refined and fastidious, you can well feel that handling other people's used sheets and dirty dishes is a bit on the unaesthetic side, while handling a hoe and the good earth and God's unsullied weeds is dainty by comparison.

Some jobs may be too heavy for most girls and others may be beyond them for lack of know-how. I, for one, am baffled by the mere thought of doing anything which requires the most meager mechanical ability. But there are few of the usual household jobs that are beyond a reasonably intelligent boy, and with the right approach, he may be proud of his accomplishments, rather than ashamed, and may look with scorn on the boys who can't do such things, although pity would be better.

In many of the situations which grownups argue and ha-

rangue and even quarrel about, there is one way to cure ourselves which seems to me should work like a charm. Let us
say you have two children, around five and seven years old.
Now, each time you and your husband (or wife) get into
some discussion, take a quiet moment when it is over and ask
yourself: If I heard the children getting excited over something like that, how would I feel? If, for instance, I heard
them arguing about whether the boy next door was eight or
nine years old, I would tell them to ask him the next time they
saw him but in the meantime keep still about it, and anyway
why on earth did they care? And you may remember that,
when they are getting all wrought up over exactly the sort of
thing that upsets their father and mother, you often say to
them: You're a big boy now; don't act like such a baby.

In many petty arguments the bugbear is the feeling of cer-
tainty that we are right and the other person is mistaken, and
for some obscure reason we can't stand this. But it should be
relatively easy to cure ourselves; we aren't babies either, and
we should be able to convince ourselves that life will go on
just the same if someone else does think that old Mr. Johnson
was ninety when he died although we know perfectly well that
he was only eighty-nine.

Controlling our indignation over an injustice done is more
difficult to cure, but if you work at it, you may be able to convince yourself that a little injustice now and then doesn't do
you any harm. You can also be sure that you are a bit prej-
udiced in your own favor, at least part of the time, and that the
other person involved is, as likely as not, going about feeling
that he is the one who is getting the maltreatment. It is also

probable that, even if he isn't, he is a person who, in general, means to be fair and considerate and isn't working his brains overtime trying to get more than he gives.

If the difficulty is within the family, it is well to keep in mind that you aren't living in a concentration camp among strangers and enemies but with people you are supposed to love. It is your own doing that the children were brought into the world and are underfoot bothering you, and your husband or wife is the person you voluntarily chose to live with, for better or worse. At those times when it is "worse," if you will use a little ingenuity you can probably make it "better."

VIII

Petty Values Belong on the Trash Pile

Though they may be quite honestly unaware of them, many people harbor some attitudes and notions that are keeping them blocked off from even beginning to find happiness.

Let's have a look at a few of these unlovely attributes: fault-finding, snobbery, gossip, prejudice, vengefulness, hypocrisy. If you don't feel that indulging in this kind of thinking makes for an unhappy frame of mind, reduce it to simple, inanimate things and see what happens:

You sit down to dinner. The roast is cooked exactly the way you like it, the salad is excellent, and so is dessert, but the potatoes are watery and the coffee is weak. Now, which makes you feel more comfortable: to keep your thoughts (and remarks) on the items you like, or those you don't care for?

You go to some gathering which includes several "grades" of people. If you talk to those whom you consider your superiors, you are probably nervous; no doubt you hope some day to be in their glorified category, and you are wondering if they are approving of you. If you talk to some man "beneath" you, you are again nervous, hoping that he and everyone around realizes that you wouldn't dream, for instance, of inviting him to your home. But when you are talking to your equals you feel easy and relaxed, so how intelligent it would be of you simply to drop the whole artificial grading system and be comfortable with everybody!

Do we need other examples? You can surely see that gossip is hitting below the belt, that prejudice is narrow and limiting, and hypocrisy is dishonest and confusing.

As to fault-finding, nowadays, most of us have heard all about not blaming the individual, and usually one is ready to have an open mind about it. But some balk at the no-praise angle; surely, they say, a child should be praised if he does something worthy in order to keep him on the right path.

It is obvious, though, that if at any one point we are the result of our inheritance plus everything that has happened to us since we were born, we are not, in a sense, responsible for our acts or attitudes, either good or bad, which would mean that praise, as well as blame, is out of order. You can't have it both ways. I realize that here I am bordering on the free-will controversy and I have no intention of getting involved in that.

The person who behaves well is likely to be loved and admired more than the one who behaves badly, so when you take away praise you aren't depriving him of the advantages that come with good behavior. This is hard on the "bad" one if it isn't his fault that he is bad, but so is it hard on the ugly little girl that she isn't admired as much as the pretty one. If you arc looking for justice and fair treatment to all, don't look on this earth; that is something God hasn't got around to yet. That is, justice as we see it, although maybe that isn't true. Another of Mother's very few admonitions was, "Don't fret; sometimes your worst luck turns out to be your best." Surprisingly often, it does turn out to be, and maybe the ugly child is getting something out of the situation which we don't know about. But neither does she, probably, and that seems a pity.

I think this no-praise-no-blame attitude is, from the point of view of your own serenity, an excellent thing to get into your system as deeply as possible. If you don't believe that people are unhappier when they are criticizing others than when they are admiring someone, try watching the expression on their faces as they talk. You will find that you can tell from the look on a person's face what kind of a remark he is going to make before he speaks, if what he is about to say has any real feeling back of it. There is no question in my mind that you aren't at your pleasantest when you are criticizing and blaming people. Impersonal analysis, of course, is quite another matter.

If you are thinking that this tolerant attitude would make us all wishy-washy or unreliable, or that the world would stand still or go backward without blame of individuals, I believe you are mistaken. You don't have to be tolerant about a deed just because you can excuse the one who does it.

There are two kinds of criticism: that which is merely dis-
passionate appraisal and the adverse variety which gets us all
stirred up. We get sort of mad at people because they have
faults. Interestingly enough, sometimes the faults which annoy us most in other people are our own worst ones.

I won't attempt to go into the reasons some of the psychologists have given for this yen to pick at other people's flaws. For
one thing, the authorities may be mistaken or may disagree,
and, for another, I know next to nothing about it. Reasons
wouldn't help us anyway unless we were going to a psycho-
analyst to get to the bottom of it, and the majority of us
aren't getting any professional treatment.

My contention is that fault-finding, or just fault-noticing, is
not a desirable frame of mind, and I think that anyone who
is addicted to it would be more comfortable if he could get
over it. When we stand and look at a flower garden there is
likely to be some beauty to delight us, but probably it isn't all
attractive. There may be a few weeds or a sickly plant or some
flowers which are beginning to fade, or others which for some
private reason of their own didn't make a satisfactory growth.
There may be only one thing, or there may be a dozen, wrong
with the garden. If you are the one who planted the garden and
it is your business to take care of it, you will, I hope, see these
blemishes and try to do something about them, but if you are
merely an onlooker and no one is asking your valuable advice,
I hope that for your own sake you will enjoy whatever beauty
is there and not allow yourself to be preoccupied and annoyed
with the bad features.

And I hope you can train yourself to do the same thing

when you let your mind wander to Mrs. A and Mrs. B. One may be too casual a housekeeper to suit your standards, but maybe she makes good biscuits. The other may talk more than her share, but once in a long time she says something worth listening to. Now if these women haven't appealed to you for help in overcoming their deficiencies, and if you aren't planning to tell them how to reform, you will probably be better off if you don't think about their shortcomings.

This runs us directly into that thing called "gossip." I just looked up the definition; among other things, Webster says "idle talk," with not a word about the talk being malicious or untrue. "Idle talk" seems to me not to cover at all what we usually mean when we say "gossip." All we have to do to find out that almost everything we say is so idle that it's not worth repeating is to spend some time with a slightly deaf person and have to say everything twice. I have always thought that gossip was more than idle, that it got its bad name by being malicious or unfounded, if not actually untrue, or at least adversely critical.

Gossip is surely talk about people, and there is no other topic more interesting to most of us. We can say just so much about things and we are through, and an exchange of ideas will often either peter out or deteriorate into handing around insults. But people are so varied and complex that we could go on and on about almost any one person, provided we had the intelligence and insight and understanding to say all there is to be said about him. Lacking these, just speculation about a person can be fascinating.

The trouble is, in talking about people our attitude tends

to be fault-finding rather than analytical. We can go into detail about what is wrong with a painting, an automobile, a garden, and we don't feel unkind because the element of blame doesn't enter in. We can take a clock apart and try to discover what's wrong with it, and nobody would dream of accusing us of being unpleasant. But just try taking a person to pieces to find out what makes him tick, or, rather, why he doesn't tick. If we do very much of that, we are going to get the reputation of being intolerant and we will probably deserve it, because unfortunately some annoyance and feeling of superiority seem to enter in when we begin pulling people apart. I think this is a pity and I wish I could live to see the day when we are competent and discriminating enough to see others' good and bad qualities as clearly as we see the attractive and unattractive features of their faces, feeling either admiration or pity or even aversion, but neither praise nor blame. Then we could freely discuss everyone we know, and I do think that human beings are the most fascinating subject there is.

Tied in with this criticism of others are snobbery and prejudice. These are very closely related, but we'll take them one at a time, beginning with snobbery. Perhaps it is true that we look down on this one and that one to bolster our self-esteem, and that people who feel inferior to some need a whole flock of others to look down on to keep them comfortable. But, unless you are simply too conceited for words, if you look down on some people don't you have to kowtow to others, and what's attractive about that unless you're a masochist? I don't know how we got saddled with snobbery, but if only we could realize how unnecessary and childish and pitiable it is we might get over it without having to understand how we became infected.

In my whole life I saw my father do only one thing which showed that he was conscious of snobbery, not in himself but as a thing which existed in the world. When he was in his eighties I was teaching English to colored men in a small night school in Harlem. One evening something happened to the heating arrangement and the room was so cold we couldn't stand it. One of the men was so disappointed that I told him if he wanted to go home with me I would give him a lesson there.

As we were going up the hall to our living room we came to my father's bedroom. The door was standing open and he was sitting there reading. He glanced up and I took my pupil in to meet him. Dad had turned his ankle and it was a little difficult for him to get to his feet, but he rose, shook hands, and chatted a moment.

Now that is interesting, I thought. For a white man he would have explained and wouldn't have risen, but to a black man he wanted to be more courteous. Dad's manner had always been so unself-consciously the same with every kind of person that one would have thought that his knowledge of snobbery was buried so deeply that it could never come to the surface.

I have no story about my mother in this respect, but years ago one of our friends made up one and those who knew Mother agreed that it was exact. If the wife of the President (or make it good—say it was the Queen of England) came into the home of anybody at all except that of a Communist and at the same time the cleaning woman entered (and why not make her colored?), and there was only one chair in the room, needless to say the chair would be offered to the Queen. But in the home of the Communist the woman who worked for a living would be the one who was asked to sit down, if he was true to his beliefs.

"If this happened in Mrs. Stout's home," said my friend, "who would get the preferred treatment? I'll tell you who. If the Queen had just come in from a long walk and her feet hurt, she would get it, but if it was at the end of the day and the cleaning woman was tired, she would be asked to sit down."

Everybody present agreed that that was what would happen, and then somebody wanted to know what Mother would do if they were both exhausted. Just then Mother came in and someone asked her, "Mrs. Stout, if the Queen of England and your cleaning woman came into your house at the same time, both tired out, and you had only one chair, what would you do?"

Missing altogether the snob angle, Mother replied, "That's not much of a problem. There's no better way of resting than lying flat on the floor."

"Well, but which one would you ask to sit down?"

Mother shrugged her shoulders.

"I suppose I'd let them work it out for themselves."

Most children are fed on snobbery of one kind or another from babyhood on, but we were unusually free from this particular branch of education. Not only were we Quakers, which is a pretty good foundation, but also our environment was ideal in this respect. Money was scarce but we were never snubbed

on account of that, probably because Dad was superintendent
of schools and in that farming area in Kansas this carried
with it enough prestige for the "best" people to accept us.
And we didn't know enough to look down on the "low" ones.

We ran into the various brands of snobbery when we moved
to Topeka and each handled it in his own fashion. Bob, for
instance, did the upper-uppers a favor and went about with
them for a while. Walt preferred the ones on the wrong side
of the tracks. Bob made some effort to drag Walt up to his
level and once, I remember, tried to persuade Walt to go with
him to some grand lady's home for tea. Walt refused.

"Why won't you come just this once?" Bob insisted. "You
might like it."

"I know damn well I won't," was the answer.

"How do you know until you've tried it?"

"Hell, I *have* tried it. I don't like tea."

Now, what's amiss with this looking up or down on people?
I like to pounce on the churchgoers first, because any defect
is more glaring if it's in people who have a definite high code of
belief. If I understand Christians, they believe that God made
the world and everyone in it. We are all His children, the
brothers and sisters of Christ, and therefore of each other.
Well, how can anyone believe in God and feel either above or
below any of His children? Can you imagine an all-knowing,
all-powerful God making some children and then saying to
Himself: I blundered on this one, and that one certainly isn't
worthy to be asked to Mrs. So-and-so's elegant home. This
specimen must by no means be sold any property in that
neighborhood, and this other one is definitely for the birds?

Even for those who aren't Christians, snobbery is to me a peculiar attitude. It is true that there are a few "lower class" people whom I wouldn't invite to dinner because I wouldn't enjoy them, but there are also some in all the other classes whom I wouldn't invite for the same reason. I am not boasting about this, I am reluctantly admitting it, for what is more bleak and barren than exclusiveness? What could be more desirable than to be equipped with the ability to get something out of everybody?

I should think any kind of snobbery would be confusing to anyone who wasn't exposed to it from birth. Take the respect for money. A novice would get all set to kowtow to anyone appreciably richer than he was, then lo and behold, he finds out that it depends on how long you've had your wealth. There are obnoxious people called *nouveau riche*, and no matter how many millions they have you must scorn them if they had the get-up to make it themselves. Having worked for it is ignoble, to say the very least.

And just when you think you have it straight in your mind, along comes somebody with practically no money at all who won't associate with certain millionaires, no matter what. These are people whose families are "old." Since we all must have come from Adam or the monkey, a person who is a little short on brains might not be able to grasp what is so outstanding about an old family. But you can take their word for it that it is quite a thing.

As for the intellectuals, their kind of snobbishness is for my money the hardest of all to comprehend, because if they are so brilliant why don't they know better than to indulge in this callow game of feeling superior?

I remember waiting for somebody once at the Civic Club many years ago. The members of this club were intellectuals, and while I sat in a corner by myself I listened to the conversation around me. The boasting of a group of the despised *nouveau riche* could hardly have sounded more crude; one of the most noticeable aspects was the way they couldn't resist talking about the important people in their little world, calling them by their first names, letting it be known (whether true or not) that they knew them personally. It was more depressing than to hear people drag in remarks about the exclusive clubs they belong to because, presumably, this Civic Club crowd actually were equipped with good minds and could conceivably have used them to better purpose.

I don't know how much satisfaction people get out of looking down on others, but I would guess that looking up might often be irksome. And completely unnecessary, for, once you decide not to have inferiors, the next step, not to have superiors, is easy. That is, do a little straight thinking. Decide that you are enough of a person in your own right not to need to bolster your opinion of yourself by feeling better than anyone else and, that accomplished, it should be easy enough not to feel below anybody. Admire others, of course, if they are worth it, but look sideways, not up.

Surely I don't have to explain that I don't think everyone is exactly alike. Some of us have more money, beauty, kindness, intelligence, tact, wit, than others. (More old family I won't concede to anybody.) And of course I don't mean that we should open our doors and invite to dinner everybody we know. But I am sorry about the false standards and the artificial reasons for deciding whether or not to ask them. I would invite anyone to my home, rich or poor, black or white, Jew or Gentile, Italian, Russian, Chinese, if I like him and think I'll enjoy him.

I feel sure that the exclusive people miss a great deal and I think those who have a prejudice against foreigners miss more than they could believe. I doubt if there is any nationality that hasn't quite a lot to offer that is particularly its own, and people who confine their contacts to their own nationalities live in an unnecessarily small world. It is for your own pleasure and for no other reason that I beg you to try to get over any prejudice and snobbishness with which your environment may have crippled you.

Etiquette is another big fly in the ointment. It isn't as stultifying as the others, but it's just so damned silly. A cartoon I particularly like shows a servant standing by a dining-room table with some dishes in her hand and looking at her mistress with a mixture of tolerance and pity on her face. And some surprise. The maid is saying, "Serve from the left and clear the table from the right? You superstitious or something, ma'am?"

A hostess will strain every nerve to have each knife, fork, and spoon placed correctly, the right wine, the correct this and that (I'm not good at giving details because I don't know what's "correct"), and then perhaps snap at her husband during the meal over some trifle and embarrass her guests. It is conceivable that she wouldn't have been tempted to be unpleasant if she hadn't got herself tense over her efforts to serve the meal "properly."

Having ignored etiquette all my life, I can't judge from experience, but from observation I must conclude that it is apt to put quite a strain on everybody. First of all, you have to find out somehow what's proper and then you must remember to do it, and by hook or crook make the family go along with you if they, too, haven't caught the disease and are disinclined to do it of their own accord. This, I should think, would add to the strain of daily living, which is already tense enough.

Close on the heels of this nervousness, apprehension would be likely to follow—fear that you've forgotten, neglected, or are ignorant of some detail. If the people you are visiting or entertaining belong to that horrible class known as your superiors (maybe your husband's job depends on how you conduct yourself), then I suppose you could get into quite a dither. Usually, though, the fear would be faint, scarcely noticeable, but no doubt getting on your nerves as a hissing radiator, which you no longer hear consciously, is apt to do.

I'm a great believer in each one of us doing his own thinking, in little things as well as big ones. If the rules tell me to put the salad on the left side of the plate and if for any reason I want to put it on the right side, I hope I shall continue to be bold and brave enough to do it my way. That is about the only rule regarding table setting that I know about (maybe they've changed it by now), and I feel as free as a bird when I disobey it. I should look up more rules and have more fun.

Freedom, that's the important thing. I once read that freedom is not a privilege, that it is a burden, but the writer claimed it is also a duty. I think I sort of halfway know what he meant, but to whatever extent I have freedom I don't feel the burden of it at all.

Perhaps it is a matter of temperament. I have heard that psychologists and educators are beginning to tell us now (after the progressive schools proved to be a disappointment) that children need discipline, need to be told what to do, and certainly some children I have seen need to be told what not to do. It surely is obvious that they require some amount of guidance, and perhaps some people never grow up and therefore need direction, someone to make their decisions for them.

Anyway, whatever it is—burden, duty, or privilege—I am heartily in favor of freedom, but perhaps I should explain that I wouldn't want it for myself if someone else had to pay for it. If I am to stay alive, somebody has to work for the food I eat, and I prefer to do that job myself. I wouldn't feel free, for instance, to bring children into the world and then abandon them; if I am going to have any relations whatever with other human beings, I wouldn't expect, or even want, to be free from any responsibility of give-and-take. Nor would I feel justified in feeding and milking the cow I own only when I was in the mood. In other words, along with freedom I would like to hang onto a little common decency and consideration of others.

And now let's have a look at our apparent thirst for vengeance and violence. I am convinced that pretending to uphold an ideal and yet making no effort to act accordingly makes for a confused and dishonest mental and emotional state, and the fact that we are doing this without realizing it seems to me

only to aggravate the conflict. The people who love their enemies on Sunday and are all out to kill them the rest of the
week are outstanding examples of that regrettable attitude.

I have been told that something like 80 per cent of our
government's total income goes to support military power,
teaching our young men to kill other men efficiently, in case
we should think it necessary and for making armaments to be
used for the same purpose. There is a basic conflict here for
anyone who is genuinely opposed to fighting—and yet most
people continue to espouse two causes: military preparation
for war—and the Christian ethic of love and forgiveness.

A few years ago Fred and I went to the movies and by mistake got there in time to see the picture which was billed "for
the kiddies." The theater was packed with children from seven
to fourteen years old, and the movie was a Western, with
guns a-popping, blood flowing, and men riding at top speed
over the great open spaces in hot pursuit of each other. The
children were enthralled, sitting forward in their seats, waiting
breathlessly for the villain to get what was coming to him.
Which he did, of course, and when someone on "our side" shot
him in the stomach, when a look of agony came on his face
and he slowly dropped his gun, clutched at the wound, fell over
and died, stretching it out to prolong the thrill, gleeful shouts
and applause came from the kiddies.

Is that bad? I don't know. But I do know that I would hate
to see any child of mine getting such thrills out of somebody's
agony. For that matter, it distressed me to see and hear the
hearty response from those little strangers.

During the Second World War, I went into a store to get a

toy for a poor little boy someone had told me about, and there wasn't one single thing to buy for him except guns, cannons, soldiers. Since toys are given to children for their enjoyment and pleasure, since all of those on sale were made so that boys could pretend to kill, what conclusion can we draw except that war is supposed to be fun?

But none of this should be surprising. We know, if we will face it, that man hasn't progressed very far. He is a hodgepodge, something fine and noble at his best, and quite unmentionable at his worst.

If we want to face things as they are and not as we wish they were, one honest, realistic glance around us will show us that human nature can, at rare moments, be sublime, but it is also weak, pitiable, petty, cruel. I wish that we could see it as it is and not mind too much. Improve it, of course, if we can, but begin at the bottom and not at the top. Which means that each of us must begin with his own small, imperfect self —a far cry from reforming the world and the whole human race in the span of one lifetime, but what is so bad about pursuing the attainable?

IX

Light Shimmering Through the Darkness

I suppose most of us would agree that it is a great convenience to have words with which to express our thoughts to others, but it does seem a pity to need so many of them to get an idea across. When I say to someone, for instance, that my conception of happiness is not a hit-and-miss affair which comes and goes as a by-product of something outside ourselves, but one which stands by us under all circumstances, he often jumps to the conclusion that I am being entirely unrealistic. He thinks that I expect this "happy person" of my imagination to go around bubbling with joy in the presence of any adversity, including his own, and of course I don't mean that;

if nothing else, I think it would be tactless to beam with pleasure in the presence of someone who is miserable, and surely impossible if we, ourselves, are the sufferers.

On the other hand, the kind of happiness I mean doesn't fly out the window the minute misfortune comes through the door. The one who has attained it can't escape physical pain, or regret when he has done something he shouldn't have, or concern when he loses his job and can't find another, or loneliness, or sorrow when someone he loves is in trouble or ill or dying, but he has built up a way of life—a philosophy, if you want to call it that—which prevents a feeling of guilt, or fruitless anxiety, or worry, or despair.

What can a happy person do to cope successfully with physical pain? Well, remember that our serene person is one who has learned to live in the moment, to a large degree has abandoned anxiety, worry, fear; I strongly suspect that there have been more painful hours spent looking forward to a visit to the dentist's, to an operation, to sickness, than have actually been endured while going through these unwelcome experiences.

I also believe that we lessen, or strengthen, our physical suffering by our thoughts, and many doctors will go along with that. Bodily pain in the middle of the night, when we are alone, is perhaps the most difficult to bear; I have been in that situation only a few times, and when I am I say to myself: Just a few more hours until morning, I can stand anything for a few hours. And it helps, too, to remind yourself: "This, too, will pass."

We have already touched on regret, and on letting it mount to a feeling of guilt, but I would like to add a word about it here, where we are considering the misfortunes that are so large that we feel it is impossible to retain any serenity. It seems to me that the biggest cause for regret that anyone could have would be that of bringing children into the world and then making a mess of raising them properly. What is "properly"? Well, I would say that you mustn't spoil them, must look after their health, give them sane values, teach them to think for themselves and not have prejudices—but, no, I am asking far too much; almost no parents are going to accomplish all that, and many wouldn't even know how to go about trying.

However, if the time should ever come when you can see clearly where you have failed your children, I don't see how you could escape having regrets. If you had done the best you could, though, or if you had been simply too weak to follow through what you felt you should do, why waste time and energy feeling guilty about it? Since it is too late to do anything toward molding the lives of your children, you can at least be careful not to repeat your mistakes—that is, not proceed to spoil your grandchildren.

Some of you may think that being out of work isn't a big enough trouble to include here with the major disasters; one can at least do something about it, you say—look for another job. True, but I am talking about the man who has trouble finding any kind of work, or the woman who has been left with two or three small children and no money. In short, about the problem of poverty, which is no joke even in these enlightened days of relief and unemployment insurance and so on. What does our "happy" person do about it?

First I am going to tell you a true story. Many years ago there was a strike in a large manufacturing plant in New Jersey. I was in sympathy with the strikers and went over there to see if there was anything I could do to help. The strike had been going on for many weeks, and I saw plenty of worry and distress and tried to do what little I could.

Meetings were called to encourage the strikers to hold out, and I attended one of them. The speaker was a man I happened to know; he was big, good-looking, well known, with a hearty manner and pleasant personality, and he was also an excellent speaker. He gave an eloquent talk and at the end of it told the tired, worried, and perhaps hungry strikers to "hold out until you starve."

Well, I knew that this man was married to a woman who had quite a lot of money and that the chances were that he would go home that evening to a more than substantial meal, and, even though he had probably put heart into those desperate people and quite likely had done a good thing, his talk made me feel a little sick. It may be a weakness on my part, but even if I knew it was sound advice, I couldn't tell anyone to go hungry while I had plenty to eat.

I was brought up in a large family where money was far from plentiful, and I am thankful for it; I am an expert at living comfortably and happily without luxuries. But I have never been in a position where I was responsible for children whom I couldn't feed adequately, and I have no intention of glibly attempting to tell a person with that problem how to take it without worry and anxiety. It is of course true that worry will hinder rather than help, and the person who has inner resources to fall back on is in a better position than one who hasn't. And he will probably find a job sooner than will the one who has let despair overtake him.

You have probably heard intolerant, flippant criticism of the behavior of some poor family uttered by someone who has never known what poverty is and how demoralizing it can be. Over thirty years ago I met a likable young woman who had been married two or three years, her husband had a good job and she enjoyed making their modest home attractive. She was well educated and intelligent, but now and then, when the occasion arose, would impatiently say of some less fortunate family, "They could at least be clean."

Then her husband got sick, and it developed that he could never work again, although he might live for many years; my friend had to take over and earn the living and also keep house. It was hard on her in some ways, but it made of her a more tolerant, more understanding person. Now and then, through those difficult years, I heard her say, "Well, I used to criticize women whose houses were dirty; now I know that cleanliness is a luxury which everybody can't afford."

The point I am trying to make is that, much more often than we know, various forms of adversity are blessings in disguise. It will do no harm, when trouble appears, to remind ourselves that for all we know this very thing we are suffering from just now may in the end be good for us, and we are fortunate if we are alert enough to make use of it to some constructive purpose.

There are two kinds of loneliness: that which comes from being physically alone, and that other one which, one hears, is the worst of all—a feeling of aloneness in the midst of a crowd. From experience I know nothing about that second variety; my guess is that it is a part of some people's temperament, or is a neurosis, such as that feeling of impending doom with which some people are cursed; even if it is as bad as that, I should think it might be possible to control it (or, rather, lessen it) to some extent by learning to crowd it out with positive thoughts.

I mentioned earlier that many years ago I read that, in times of stress, it is a great help to force ourselves to dwell on something outside our suffering, if only for a fraction of a minute; this is supposed to bring at least some small relief. If that is true, I should think it would be relatively easy, if you were lonely in the midst of a crowd, to snatch one moment after another and instead of gloomily thinking: Oh, how lonely I am! look around you and say to yourself, "That man seems to be in love with that girl," or "Why on earth would any woman buy a hat like that?", and so on. And you might even spy another person who looks desolate, and strike up an acquaintance, thus doing a good turn to another as well as yourself. But whatever you turn your thoughts to, even if it should be only impatient criticism of everyone around you (which, in itself, isn't very gay), it would probably be better than dwelling on your misery.

A great many people who live alone can tell you things that are both good and bad about it. For instance, if they get depressed there is no one around for whom they have to try to be cheerful. Some women will say that they hate to cook only for themselves, and to eat alone. A man is likely to feel lost without someone to go home to who will listen to his new project, or his small troubles, or to laugh at his jokes. Many people turn on the radio or television primarily to hear a human voice, and I suppose a person could get so desperate that even the sound of a commercial would be better than nothing.

What can we do about this kind of loneliness? I should think it might be profitable to dwell on its advantages rather than on the opposite. I know people who are living alone and not liking it, but who will admit, if pinned down, that it is more desirable than having to adjust to another person. And the difference in freedom is tremendous; if you haven't a job you can get up and go to bed when you wish, go out if you feel like it, stay at home if you prefer that. But I surely don't have to make a list. And if you do have to go to a job—well, I should think that, after having been with people all day long, you might be glad of a little respite.

In any case, the probabilities are that you aren't obliged to live alone; if you really minded it as much as some people say they do, you could probably find someone to share your home. So choose the lesser of two evils, then dwell on its advantages rather than on its undesirable aspects.

There is this, too, about it: sometimes we need to be alone, at other times we prefer not to be. If you are living with other people (particularly your husband or your wife), it is often impossible to get off to yourself at a moment's notice, when you happen to wish you could. But if you're living alone and feel in the mood for contact with other human beings, you can usually manage it, one way or another. The various means for getting in touch with our fellow creatures are almost endless,

if we really want to, and if we haven't lived in such a way
that it is easy to form some kind of relationship with other
people, perhaps it is high time we began to learn that art.
Providing, of course, that we feel the need of it.

In a way I feel that the serious illness or suffering of those
near to us is harder to bear philosophically than our own; I
suppose we manage to feel a bit noble and courageous when
we take our own troubles with fortitude, but almost callous
when we contrive to bear another's misfortunes gallantly. In
any case, if we live very long we are going to be obliged to face
adversity, both our own and that of others, so it is worth the
effort to build up some capacity to meet it.

Let's imagine that we have a liking for growing vegetables
and flowers. After we have done this for a few years we realize
that there will never be a season when everything will come
out perfectly; no matter how much we learn, or whatever we
do, one year will be bad for tomatoes, another for verbenas,
another for the cabbage family, and so on. Each growing season brings its disappointment. For instance, everything is going along splendidly and you really think this is going to be the
perfect season, then you go out one morning and find that the
raccoons have taken your corn, although you were sure you had
it adequately protected. This is a disaster because corn is your
favorite crop, yet you don't go to pieces, for another year is
coming and in the meantime you may think up an adequate
way to defeat the marauders.

And so with life. If you are only slightly realistic, you will
accept the fact that here and there misfortune will overtake
you, that almost any dreadful thing can happen to you, or to

the ones you love best. But if you aren't willing to admit defeat, if you are determined to outwit the raccoons and have some corn next year, you will put your mind to work and do something about it. And if you don't intend to let some almost overwhelming sorrow spoil your life, you will build up day by day an inner strength, an ability to live in the moment, a gift for making the most of the good things that are all around you, instead of indulging in self-pity and despair.

Death has taken away several people who were dear to me—two sisters, two brothers, my mother and father—but at the time of their going I wasn't living with any of them and this makes a difference. Many times through the day you will think of them with sadness, but at least every small thing around you doesn't remind you of them. Then, recently, I lost my husband; for over four months he was distressingly ill, very depressed, and longing to die, and no doubt it was a good thing for me that he required almost constant care, for although it wore me out physically, I at least had no time to sit and contemplate my sorrow. When you are faced with only two alternatives—one, seeing someone you love suffer and the other, losing him—the situation is indeed desperate, and you are lucky if you have no time for dwelling on it.

Then Fred died and I was alone, and every single thing in the house had its memory of him. There was the large leather chair, which was so completely his that I had scarcely ever sat in it through the twenty-odd years we had had it. Was the sight of it, day after day, going to be painful? Should I give it away? But why, when there was no possible way of escaping the memories which everything else around me emphasized, unless I simply walked out and left everything behind me?

Now I had a choice: I could dwell on my loss, could weep over the things Fred had enjoyed, reproach myself when I looked at the table he had made and had finished so beautifully, and which I hadn't kept polished as well as he would have liked me to, or I could count my blessings. There were two of these that called for gratitude, and one was that Fred was no longer suffering; he was almost seventy-nine, and when we get to that age we become used to the realization that we probably won't be around much longer, so that the thought of dying, although inevitably a shock for the ones who are left behind, isn't devastating. The other blessing was that Fred had gone first; before he became ill we had talked about what it would be like if one of us was left alone, and we both hoped that I would be that one, for we both knew it would be much harder for Fred to cope with the problems of everyday living by himself. So I felt I would be ungrateful indeed if I sat around and complained when we got our wish.

I suppose gratitude that things are no worse than they are is a negative attitude, yet I can find nothing wrong with it. If you are right-handed and break your left wrist, you can be thankful it wasn't your right one, and if you should break your right arm, you can think how lucky you are that it wasn't a leg or hip or your back; when I fell on the ice last winter and realized that my arm was badly hurt, I managed, even before I got to my feet, to give thanks that it wasn't my leg—that I didn't have to lie there and freeze before anyone found me.

But to return to that more serious problem of facing a life alone, it always comes back to the same panacea: pleasant thinking. And manage to keep busy at something that interests you, and not merely for the sake of keeping in motion; you can be as depressed while hemming a dress or driving a nail as you can just sitting in a chair, brooding. Remind yourself that if you cared enough, you could find someone to live with you, and usually you will have to admit that you don't want that; you have made a choice, and if you feel you must be sorry for somebody, put your mind on the unfortunate people who are living with someone and wish they weren't, but for one reason or another can't escape.

Unless you are very old you can begin now, before adversity overtakes you, to put both small and large interests into your daily life, build the habit of paying attention to the world around you, whether just in your own vicinity or in the wide world. If, however, you are quite aged and feel it is too late to start afresh, get what comfort you can in the thought that you can take whatever comes, simply because you must.

Sit back in your chair, feeling perhaps lonely, miserable, depressed, and glance at the clock and listen to its ticking. Time goes forward, forward, and nothing can stop it, and you go with it. Minute after minute passes and now an hour has gone by, for just a while ago it was three o'clock and now it is four. So you managed to live through that hour, and you no doubt will survive the next one, and the next, and, though you may not like them, you will learn to bear them. That's not a very gay way to live through the days, but I have made it grim on purpose. It is a plea to you who haven't reached this desperate stage to get busy now and live in such a way that you will never reach it.

X

And Now You Have Earned the Right to Dream

You who believe that happiness is merely a by-product of something else have probably already forsaken me. And the ones who agree with me in theory but can't get serious about learning to control their irritability, can't abandon the need to do what everyone else is doing, who must compete and "get ahead," who can't free themselves from the longing for unnecessary material possessions—well, they probably haven't had time to read this far.

The hypocrites, whether conscious or unconscious, no doubt

deserted me long ago. And the adolescents, who have put suffering on a pedestal, and particularly the oversophisticated,
who think that any effort to find happiness is corny—well,
Pascal comments on their sophomoric attitudes far more effectively than I can, and more dogmatically than I dare. He
says: "All men seek happiness. This is without exception.
Whatever different means they employ they all tend to this
end. The cause of some going to war and others avoiding it is
the same desire in both attended with different views. The
will never takes the least step but to this object. This is the
motive of every action of every man, even of those who hang
themselves."

Once more let's reduce the thing to simple terms. However
much a person may scorn the concept of pursuing happiness,
I believe he would rather feel good than miserable; let's take
our supercilious friend, who despises the "simple" folk who
admit that above all they would like to be happy, and follow
him through two days of his life.

On the one morning he gets up feeling fit, and he isn't
rushed—has time for a second cup of coffee, which tastes unusually good. It's a fine bracing morning and he goes to his job
and everything progresses smoothly; his co-workers are pleasant, his boss praises him for something well done. He goes to
lunch with someone who looks up to him and he has a pleasant time. That evening he has a dinner and theater engagement with the girl he likes best; the food is excellent, his
companion sparkling, and, if you can believe it, he is unable to
find any fault with the play.

I needn't go into detail about the second day, but he has

nervous indigestion, breakfast coffee is weak, boss is cranky—everything in reverse. Now, unless our young man is neurotic to the point of being better off in a mental institution, he would prefer, if he had a choice, the pleasant day to the other one; in other words, he likes to be "happy" although he would never be caught admitting it. And while it's true that both days are accidental, it's also true that, given a little thought and effort, they needn't be. Once we admit that we would rather have pleasant days than unpleasant ones, and realize that we aren't such weaklings that we can do nothing about achieving this, we have taken the first step toward ruling our life instead of letting it rule us.

Not even the most experienced architect can take a pencil and erect a finished house, but a humble worker, laying brick on brick, can accomplish it in time. And he doesn't achieve this by accident, he has to learn how and must use his brains as well as his hands.

It is the same with pleasant hours; an accidental one now and then is welcome, but you can't rely on them when you most need them. Just as a builder must see to it that his structure won't tumble to the ground with the first storm, so you too must learn how to build a life that doesn't fall to pieces in the face of every big and little misfortune which will confront you.

And now my last word is for those of you who agree with me to some extent, who believe that we can refuse to live a petty, tense, cluttered life, full of wrangling, fault-finding, worry, depression, hypocrisy, loneliness, boredom, and despair. And especially for you who have figured out how to shape your days and years into cheering ones which you can depend on; I am glad for you and everyone around you. And, since you have done so much and have done it so well, I have a further suggestion: why not do a bit of dreaming, hitch your wagon to that star again, and have a little fun pursuing the unattainable?

Printed in the USA
CPSIA information can be obtained
at www.ICGtesting.com
LVHW090535141124
796586LV00005B/50